WALKS ON THE
NORTH YORK MOORS

30 SHORT CIRCULAR WALKS
OF
OUTSTANDING BEAUTY AND INTEREST

JACK KEIGHLEY

WESTERDALE CHURCH   WALK 19

WALKS ON THE
NORTH YORK MOORS

an illustrated guide to thirty walks
of outstanding beauty and interest

by

J Keighley

CICERONE PRESS
POLICE SQUARE, MILNTHORPE

ISBN 1 85284 134 6

Also by *JKeighley*

WALKS IN THE YORKSHIRE DALES
ISBN 1 85284 034 X

**WALKS IN THE YORKSHIRE DALES
BOOK TWO**
ISBN 1 85284 065 X

**WALKS IN THE YORKSHIRE DALES
BOOK THREE**
ISBN 1 85284 085 4

WALKS IN LANCASHIRE WITCH COUNTRY
ISBN 1 85284 093 5

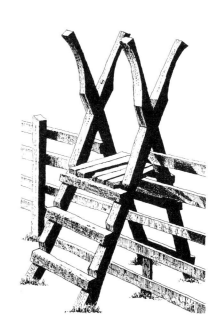

INTRODUCTION

On the 28th. November 1952 North East Yorkshire's marvellous purple acres of heather moorland became the sixth area of outstanding natural beauty in England and Wales to be designated as a National Park.

The North York Moors National Park covers an area of 553 sq. miles, and is bounded on three sides by vast lowland plains. To the north and west lie, respectively, the Cleveland Plain and the Vale of Mowbray, from which the moors rise in sudden, dramatic escarpments, whilst to the south-west and south are the fertile Vales of York and Pickering. Twenty-five miles of spectacular, rocky North Sea coastline forms the Park's eastern boundary. The two main aims of the National Park Authorities are a) to preserve and enhance the natural beauty of the Park and b) to encourage the provision or improvement of facilities for the enjoyment of open-air recreation and the study of nature within the Park.

Moors, dales and coastline constitute the three basic elements of the National Park, but its boundaries embrace an incredibly diverse range of distinctive features :-

- the country's greatest expanse of heather moorland
- undulating agricultural land
- broad, pastoral dales and steep, wooded valleys
- precipitous sea-cliffs and delightful rocky bays with golden sands
- beautiful natural woodlands and extensive tracts of dark coniferous plantations
- lazy, meandering rivers and rushing moorland streams
- ten nature reserves
- fifty-three Sites of Special Scientific Interest
- palatial homes and stately mansions
- remote, sleepy hamlets, bustling market towns and quaint fishing villages
- relics of ancient civilizations
- fascinating remains of former industries
- glorious abbeys, venerable churches and hoary old castles
- imaginative museums and visitor centres
- one of the country's finest preserved steam railways

Riches a-plenty, to which an intricate network of country roads gives easy access. When one also considers that within the Park are over 1000 miles of public bridleways and footpaths – not to mention old drovers' roads, paved packhorse trods, old railway trackbeds, forestry paths and waymarked trails – it is little wonder that the area is regarded as one of Britain's finest walking locations, or that over 11,000,000 good souls come a-visiting each year.

The basic bedrock of the moors was formed in the shallow seas of the Jurassic period over 150 million years ago. Some 80 million years ago stresses and pressures in the earth's crust forced up the ocean floor to create what geologists call 'The Cleveland Dome'. The 'dome has subsequently been subjected to the continuous erosion by wind, water and ice which has shaped the landscape to its present configuration. The old Jurassic rocks are visible on the sides of the dales and particularly along the coast, where savage and remorseless erosion by the North Sea has created a geologist's paradise. The northern moors have a capping of sandstone, whilst limestone is evident to the south.

Though nature has shaped these moors and dales, it is the influence of man which has largely created the landscape which we see today. The earliest signs thus far discovered of human activity on the moors date back some 5,000 years. During the Bronze Age (3,000 years ago) much of the natural forest was cleared, and large numbers of 'barrows' or burial mounds (often named on maps as 'howes') were constructed. The Romans built a road to the coast, and established a series of signal stations to warn of impending naval invasion. The coming of Christianity saw the erection of numerous moorland and wayside crosses. The region is famous for these, and one of them – Young Ralph Cross – was chosen to be the emblem of the National Park. The 11th. and 12th. centuries witnessed the founding of many fine abbeys (earlier ones had been destroyed by Viking marauders). Huge and prosperous monastic estates developed, and vast numbers of sheep grazed the moors, thereby preventing the natural regeneration of woodland. In more recent times widespread mining and quarrying activity in pursuit of such minerals as alum, ironstone, jet, coal, potash and salt has left its mark. The necessity of transporting goods to and from the coast created a network of flagged packhorse trods. In 1920 the Forestry Commission arrived with their conifers, which today occupy about 15% of the Park's total acreage.

My aim in writing this introduction has been to attempt a general description of the superb countryside which the lucky user of this book may expect to enjoy, and the major factors which have shaped and fashioned it. Researching and recording these walks has, despite the weather(*), given me a huge amount of pleasure, and my sincere wish is that you may derive equal enjoyment in following my footsteps.   Happy Walking.

JKeighley

January 1993

* Several consulted books insist that the North York Moors has the lowest annual rainfall of all our upland Parks. The author, having spent the whole of 1992 walking these routes in almost incessant rain – and exceedingly wet rain – remains unconvinced of the veracity of this assertion.

ABOUT THIS BOOK

THE WALKS All the walks described in this book are circular, and begin at a place where a car may be parked without causing an obstruction. They are fairly uniform in length, an average of 6¼ miles making them half-day rather than full-day excursions. The selected walks lie almost entirely within the boundaries of the North York Moors National Park, and collectively they incorporate every type of landscape to be found in this beautiful region – riverside meadows, natural woodland, planted forest, coastal cliffs, limestone and gritstone scars and crags, steep escarpments and – above all – rolling acres of superb heather moorland. The routes adhere almost exclusively to public rights-of-way, with occasional recourse to commonly-used tracks in open country. They should be free from serious difficulty, and well within the capability of reasonably fit and agile walkers.

THE MAPS The strip-maps show all relevant route-finding features. All the routes have been walked and surveyed in detail by the author, and great care has been taken to ensure accuracy, although for the sake of clarity there is deliberate distortion of scale in depicting routes along, for example, narrow lanes or through farmyards. Changes, however, will occur quite frequently, particularly on low-level routes across farmland, where the walker may expect to encounter new stiles and fences, and also diversions, either temporary or permanent. In such cases please note and obey legitimate waymarks and signs. In the Route Directions any mention of a gate, stile or footbridge means that it is used, unless otherwise stated. The maps and route directions together should suffice to make it quite clear to you how you've got lost. It is strongly recommended that an Ordnance Survey map be carried, as this will add interest and enable the walker to identify distant features not mentioned in the text.

WALKING IN THE NATIONAL PARK

A FEW WORDS OF ADVICE

● Many of the routes in this book cross agricultural land, and farmers will not welcome inconsiderate visitors. When crossing fields keep closely to paths, and walk in single file across meadowland. Avoid climbing walls, and securely close all gates behind you (unless they are obviously meant to be left open)

● Leave no litter.

● Dogs must be kept on a lead in the proximity of livestock. This is especially vital during lambing time (March to May).

● Cars must not be parked where they obstruct field gates or cause damage to grass verges. Lock your car securely and hide from view any attractive or valuable items (or take them with you).

● Some of the routes described in this book cross high, exposed moorland terrain where weather conditions may be less pleasant than at valley level. Should the weather turn nasty, don't hesitate to call it a day and return by the route along which you came.

● When walking along a motor road walk on the right to face the oncoming traffic. The exception to this is on approaching a blind bend, where it may be necessary to cross to the left for a clear view.

● Before setting out, try to let others know where you're going (especially if you're walking alone).

CLOTHING AND EQUIPMENT Boots or strong, comfortable shoes are essential (on the high moors and in winter boots are the only suitable footwear). A windproof jacket or anorak (preferably with a hood) will be needed. Thick, heavy sweaters are not recommended – two or three lightweight layers are warmer and more adaptable to changing conditions. Denim is not at all suitable. In cold weather a woollen hat or cap will prevent the loss of a great deal of body heat.

A walking-stick is a matter of personal preference. Some walkers wouldn't be seen dead with one, but the author's constant companion is a hazel knobstick, which he finds useful for very steep, slippery descents, fording streams, beating down nettles, discouraging aggressive animals and testing potentially boggy ground prior to sinking in up to the knees. (A stick can be a nuisance on a route which involves steep

8

rock - scrambling, but there are none of those in this book). A rucsac is needed. A small 'daysac' with a capacity of about 20 litres would be adequate for any of these walks. The author's rucsac will always contain the following items : —

- waterproof cagoule and overtrousers
- spare woollen pullover
- small first - aid kit
- large - scale O.S. map
- compass
- whistle
- plastic bottle for water or cold drink
- a high - calorie snack (usually chocolate or crisps)
- windproof lighter for getting the old briar going (the alternative being about ten boxes of matches)

To these basic items may be added a pair of gloves and a flask containing hot coffee or soup.

CHILDREN When taking children on country walks some thought must be given to the distance and the type of terrain involved. Until you are sure of the child's capabilities, keep the distances short. Most of the walks in this book would probably be too much for a child under the age of five. As a rough rule of thumb, a child should be able to manage about a mile for each year of his age after his fifth birthday. Children should be warmly clothed and well shod. One cannot always afford to buy expensive boots for growing feet, but at least the child should have strong shoes or close - fitting wellingtons. On no account should young children be allowed to wander off beyond the range of vision of responsible adults, and extreme care and control must be exercised in the vicinity of crags, quarries, old mine workings and motor roads.

THE WALKS

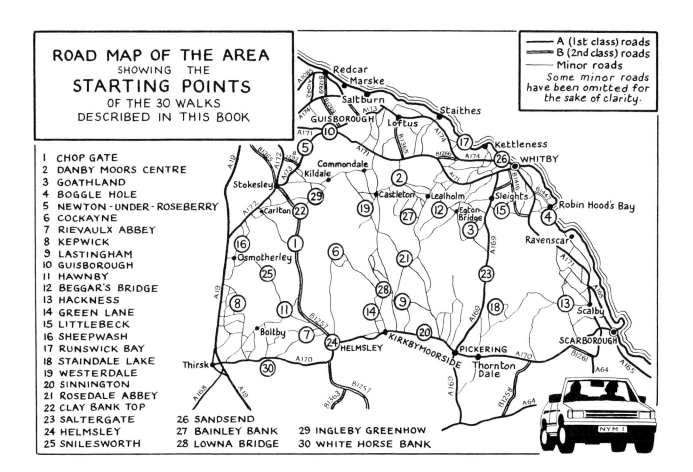

ROAD MAP OF THE AREA
SHOWING THE
STARTING POINTS
OF THE 30 WALKS
DESCRIBED IN THIS BOOK

— A (1st class) roads
⹀ B (2nd class) roads
— Minor roads
Some minor roads have been omitted for the sake of clarity.

1 CHOP GATE
2 DANBY MOORS CENTRE
3 GOATHLAND
4 BOGGLE HOLE
5 NEWTON-UNDER-ROSEBERRY
6 COCKAYNE
7 RIEVAULX ABBEY
8 KEPWICK
9 LASTINGHAM
10 GUISBOROUGH
11 HAWNBY
12 BEGGAR'S BRIDGE
13 HACKNESS
14 GREEN LANE
15 LITTLEBECK
16 SHEEPWASH
17 RUNSWICK BAY
18 STAINDALE LAKE
19 WESTERDALE
20 SINNINGTON
21 ROSEDALE ABBEY
22 CLAY BANK TOP
23 SALTERGATE
24 HELMSLEY
25 SNILESWORTH

26 SANDSEND
27 BAINLEY BANK
28 LOWNA BRIDGE

29 INGLEBY GREENHOW
30 WHITE HORSE BANK

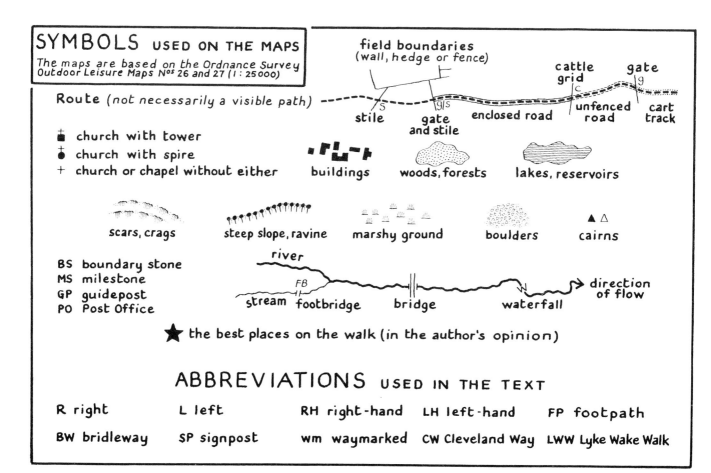

SYMBOLS USED ON THE MAPS

The maps are based on the Ordnance Survey Outdoor Leisure Maps Nos 26 and 27 (1:25000)

field boundaries (wall, hedge or fence)

cattle grid

gate

Route (*not necessarily a visible path*)

stile

gate and stile

enclosed road

unfenced road

cart track

- ▮ church with tower
- ● church with spire
- + church or chapel without either

buildings

woods, forests

lakes, reservoirs

scars, crags

steep slope, ravine

marshy ground

boulders

cairns

BS boundary stone
MS milestone
GP guidepost
PO Post Office

river

FB

stream

footbridge

bridge

waterfall

direction of flow

★ the best places on the walk (in the author's opinion)

ABBREVIATIONS USED IN THE TEXT

R right   L left   RH right-hand   LH left-hand   FP footpath

BW bridleway   SP signpost   wm waymarked   CW Cleveland Way   LWW Lyke Wake Walk

INFORMATION CENTRES

DANBY : The Moors Centre, Danby YO21 2NB. (0287) 660654. Open April–October, every day, 10–5. November–March, weekends only, 11–4.

SUTTON BANK : National Park Centre, Sutton Bank, Thirsk YO7 2EK. (0845) 597426. Open April–October, every day, 10–5. November–March, weekends only, 11–4.

HELMSLEY : Information Centre, Market Place. (0439) 70173. Open April–October, every day, 9·30–6. November–March, weekends only, 9·30–4.

GREAT AYTON : High Green car park. (0642) 722835. Open Easter–Oct., Mon–Sat, 10–4, Sun 1–4.

GUISBOROUGH : Fountain St., (0287) 633801. Open Mar–Oct., every day, 9–5. Nov–Mar, Tue–Sat 9–5.

HUTTON–LE–HOLE : Ryedale Folk Museum. (07515) 367. Open Mar 29–Nov 1, every day, 10–5·30.

LOW DALBY : Forestry Commission, Low Dalby, Pickering. (0751) 60295. Open Mar 20–Apr 30, every day, 11–4. May–Oct, every day, 10–5·30. Nov., weekends only, 11–4.

PICKERING : Eastgate car park. (0751) 73791. Open Mar–Oct., every day, 9·30–6. Nov–Feb., Mon–Sat., 10–4·30.

RAVENSCAR : NT Coastal Centre. (0723) 870138. Open weekends and Bank Holidays, Apr, May and Sep, 10·30–5·30. May 27–Aug 31, every day, 10·30–5·30.

SCARBOROUGH : St. Nicholas Cliff (0723) 373333. Open May–Sep, Mon–Sat., 9–7·30, Sun 9–5·30. Oct–Apr, every day, 9–5·30

WHITBY : Lambourn Rd., (0947) 602674. Open May–Sep, Mon–Sat., 9–6·30, Sun 9–5·30. Oct–Apr, every day, 9–5·30

①

THE SUMMIT OF THE NORTH YORK MOORS

8½ MILES

A long, gentle climb to the O.S. column on Urra Moor which, at 1489', marks the National Park's highest point. The broadness of the summit detracts from its merit as a viewpoint, but, by way of compensation, the two sections of the walk which follow the line of an ancient dyke along the moor's western brink offer superb views into and across Bilsdale.

JKeighley

summit of Urra Moor

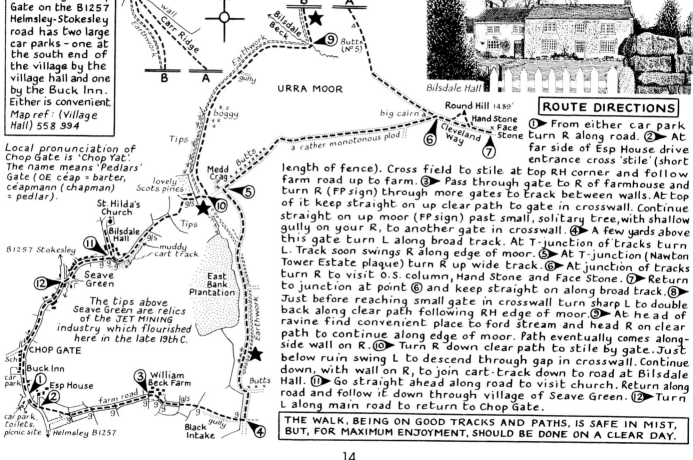

PARKING The small village of Chop Gate on the B1257 Helmsley-Stokesley road has two large car parks – one at the south end of the village by the village hall and one by the Buck Inn. Either is convenient. Map ref: (Village Hall) 558 994

Local pronunciation of Chop Gate is 'Chop Yat'. The name means 'Pedlars' Gate (OE céap = barter, céapmann (chapman) = pedlar).

N

wall

Carr Ridge

Earthwork

B · A

Earthwork

gully

boggy

Tips

Butts

lovely Scots pines

Medd Crag

St. Hilda's Church

Bilsdale Hall

muddy cart track

B1257 Stokesley

Seave Green

The tips above Seave Green are relics of the JET MINING industry which flourished here in the late 19th C.

Tips

East Bank Plantation

Earthwork

CHOP GATE

Sch

Buck Inn

car park

Esp House

car park, toilets, picnic site ↓ Helmsley B1257

farm road

William Beck Farm

Black Intake

gully

Butts

URRA MOOR

Bilsdale Beck

Butts (No 5)

a rather monotonous plod

big cairn △

Round Hill 1489'

Hand Stone
× Face Stone

Cleveland Way

Bilsdale Hall

ROUTE DIRECTIONS

① From either car park turn R along road. ② At far side of Esp House drive entrance cross 'stile' (short length of fence). Cross field to stile at top RH corner and follow farm road up to farm. ③ Pass through gate to R of farmhouse and turn R (FP sign) through more gates to track between walls. At top of it keep straight on up clear path to gate in crosswall. Continue straight on up moor (FP sign) past small, solitary tree, with shallow gully on your R, to another gate in crosswall. ④ A few yards above this gate turn L along broad track. At T-junction of tracks turn L. Track soon swings R along edge of moor. ⑤ At T-junction (Nawton Tower Estate plaque) turn R up wide track. ⑥ At junction of tracks turn R to visit O.S. column, Hand Stone and Face Stone. ⑦ Return to junction at point ⑥ and keep straight on along broad track. ⑧ Just before reaching small gate in crosswall turn sharp L to double back along clear path following RH edge of moor. ⑨ At head of ravine find convenient place to ford stream and head R on clear path to continue along edge of moor. Path eventually comes alongside wall on R. ⑩ Turn R down clear path to stile by gate. Just below ruin swing L to descend through gap in crosswall. Continue down, with wall on R, to join cart-track down to road at Bilsdale Hall. ⑪ Go straight ahead along road to visit church. Return along road and follow it down through village of Seave Green. ⑫ Turn L along main road to return to Chop Gate.

THE WALK, BEING ON GOOD TRACKS AND PATHS, IS SAFE IN MIST, BUT, FOR MAXIMUM ENJOYMENT, SHOULD BE DONE ON A CLEAR DAY.

14

Hand Stone

The SUMMIT of Urra Moor, and the highest point of the North York Moors, is known as ROUND HILL or BOTTON HEAD. As a viewpoint it comes as something of a disappointment, for the broad top of the moor allows no depth to the picture in any direction. Nearby are two interesting waymarker stones. The HAND STONE has hands pointing east - 'THIS IS THE WAY TO KIR' (Kirbymoorside) and west - 'THIS IS THE WAY TO STO' (Stokesley). It was probably placed here following a meeting

Face Stone

of magistrates at Northallerton on 2nd October 1711, when an order was made for guideposts to be erected throughout the North Riding. The FACE STONE is even more ancient, for it was mentioned in a boundary survey carried out in 1642.

Urra Moor Dyke
This ancient ditch and bank earthwork extends for some 3 miles along the rim of Urra Moor's steep western declivity, holding a level course at about 1,100'. Dry-stone walling is visible in the rampart, which is up to 12' wide and 9' high. The earthwork, known locally as 'Cromwell's Trenches', is of unknown age and purpose.

SCOTS PINE (Pinus sylvestris)
Some fine specimens of this lovely tree will be seen on the walk. It is the only native British pine, and is planted for both commercial and decorative reasons. The green cones turn brown when mature, and open to release winged, wind-borne seeds. The Scots Pine may live for over 200 years and attain a height of up to 120 feet.

O.S. MAPS : Landranger Series (1 : 50 000) Sheets 93 (Middlesbrough and Darlington) and 100 (Malton and Pickering) Outdoor Leisure 26 (1 : 25 000) NW and SW Sheets

© Jack Keighley 1993

②

DANBY BEACON & CLITHER BECK

7 MILES

This grand walk begins at the excellent Moors Centre and proceeds easily by way of pleasant Esk Valley lanes and pastures to the heathery slopes of Lealholm Moor. Here we visit the famous Danby Beacon, one of the Park's finest viewpoints. A detour around the exquisite little valley of Clither Beck provides a most attractive finish to this satisfying ramble.

weir, Clither Beck

JKeighley

PARKING Car park at Danby Moors Centre. Map ref: 718 084 | **ROUTE DIRECTIONS** ①► From car park turn L along road. ②► Take fence stile (FP sign) on L and cross field diagonally to stile at top corner. Go forward to farm and up cart track to L of it. Straight on through next farmyard. ③► Straight ahead along lane to Houlsyke and continue along road through village. ④► At seat and litter-bin cross ladder-stile (FP sign) and head R to stile by double power-line pole. Bear L up next field to gate in wall. Follow wall on R towards farm. ⑤► Just before reaching farm bear L up walled track. At top of it turn R over stile and descend to farm level. ⑥► On your L are two gates. Take RH (lower) one. At end of walled track go straight on through gap (not gate) in wall and follow wall on R. ⑦► At ruin turn L (wm) up field. Keep L of wall corner then go R over stile (wm). Pass to L of derelict farm and straight on over stile (wm) and across two fields. ⑧► At end of second field don't cross stile. Turn L up cart track, and at guidepost turn R to wall-stile. Follow edge of wood to foot-bridge. ⑨► Immediately across bridge go through gate on L and turn R to climb by tiny stream, through gateway in crosswall and up to gate at top of next field. Turn R along road. ⑩► Turn L at FP sign opposite farm drive, climb moor to reach wide crosstrack and follow it L to Danby Beacon. ⑪► Straight on down road (SP Danby, Castleton). ⑫► At road fork turn R (BW sign) to follow broad track in heather. Keep to main track. ⑬► On reaching fence (near a ruin) turn sharp L to double back on clear path with wall on R. From wall corner path descends gradually R to beck. Follow beckside path down to footbridge. ⑭► Cross bridge and follow green path as it bears R away from beck to pass through gate in crosswall. When it eventually peters out, keep on up to crosswall. Turn L to gate into wood and descend to Moors Centre.

Stump Cross   obviously of great antiquity

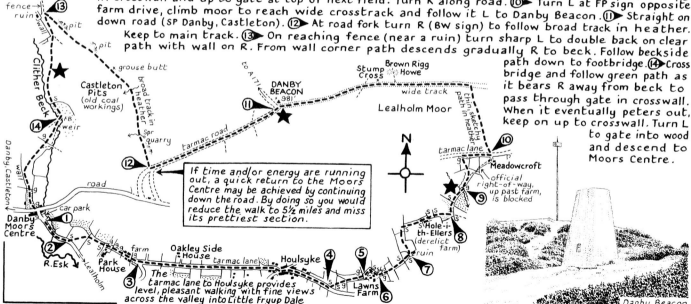

fence ruin ⑬

Clither Beck

× pit

× pit

× grouse butt

★

Castleton Pits (old coal workings)

broad track in heather

Spr

quarry

Danby Castleton

⑭ FB weir

g

g

road

g

car park

⑫

Danby Moors Centre

①

②

R. Esk

Lealholm

Park House

③

farm

Oakley Side House tarmac lane

The tarmac lane to Houlsyke provides level, pleasant walking with fine views across the valley into Little Fryup Dale

Houlsyke

Lawns Farm

④

⑤

⑥

⑦

to A171

DANBY BEACON 981'

⑪

★

Brown Rigg Howe

Stump Cross

wide track

Lealholm Moor

tarmac road

thin sketchy path in heather

⑩

tarmac lane

Meadowcroft

official right-of-way, up past farm, is blocked

⑨

g

★

⑧

Hole-i-th-Ellers (derelict farm) ruin

g

g

g

N

If time and/or energy are running out, a quick return to the Moors Centre may be achieved by continuing down the road. By doing so you would reduce the walk to 5½ miles and miss its prettiest section.

Danby Beacon

During the 18th and 19th centuries CASTLETON PITS provided coal for the burning of agricultural lime.

Hole-i-th-Ellers - a deserted farmstead

DANBY BEACON

is the National Park's supreme viewpoint north of the River Esk. The extensive panorama includes Scaling Reservoir and Boulby Potash Mine (N), R.A.F. Fylingdales (SE), the Fryup Dales and the high moors (S), Bilsdale T.V. mast (SW), Cook's Monument (W) and Teesside (NW). The pole, which stands on a Bronze Age burial mound, is a replica of a Napoleonic Wars (early 19th.C) signalling beacon.

The excellent MOORS CENTRE was created in 1976 in a building which was originally a shooting lodge. Beautifully situated by the River Esk, the Centre boasts an impressive range of resources, including tourist information, shop, displays, café, educational facilities, adventure playground, formal gardens and picnic areas. Open April–October every day 10am–5pm. November–March weekends only 11am–4pm.

Danby Moors Centre

O.S.MAPS : Landranger Series (1:50 000) Sheet 94 (Whitby)
Outdoor Leisure 27 (1:25 000) NE Sheet.

3

GOATHLAND & THE ROMAN ROAD

7½ MILES

A varied and enthralling excursion from one of the area's best-loved villages. The many highlights include the exciting river scenery of West Beck's colourful, wooded gorge, two markedly contrasting waterfalls, an extraordinarily well-preserved section of Roman road, the line of an infamous railway incline and magnificent views across rolling heather moorland.

West Beck

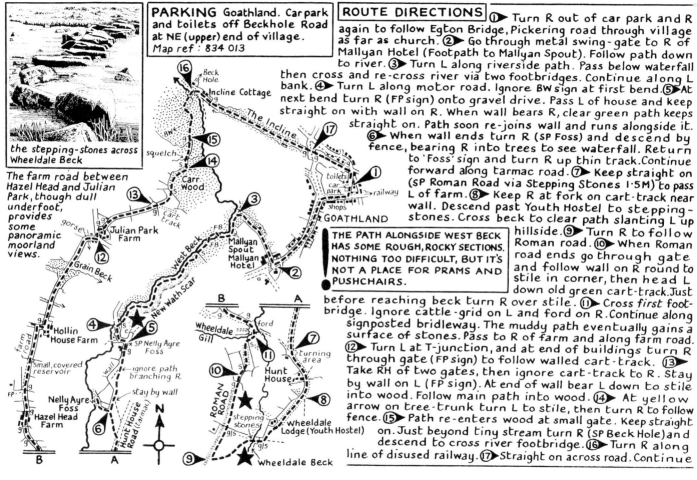

the stepping-stones across Wheeldale Beck

The farm road between Hazel Head and Julian Park, though dull underfoot, provides some panoramic moorland views.

PARKING Goathland. Car park and toilets off Beckhole Road at NE (upper) end of village. Map ref : 834 013

ROUTE DIRECTIONS

①▶ Turn R out of car park and R again to follow Egton Bridge, Pickering road through village as far as church. ②▶ Go through metal swing-gate to R of Mallyan Hotel (Footpath to Mallyan Spout). Follow path down to river. ③▶ Turn L along riverside path. Pass below waterfall then cross and re-cross river via two footbridges. Continue along L bank. ④▶ Turn L along motor road. Ignore BW sign at first bend. ⑤▶ At next bend turn R (FP sign) onto gravel drive. Pass L of house and keep straight on with wall on R. When wall bears R, clear green path keeps straight on. Path soon re-joins wall and runs alongside it. ⑥▶ When wall ends turn R (SP Foss) and descend by fence, bearing R into trees to see waterfall. Return to 'Foss' sign and turn R up thin track. Continue forward along tarmac road. ⑦▶ Keep straight on (SP Roman Road via Stepping Stones 1·5M) to pass L of farm. ⑧▶ Keep R at fork on cart-track near wall. Descend past Youth Hostel to stepping-stones. Cross beck to clear path slanting L up hillside. ⑨▶ Turn R to follow Roman road. ⑩▶ When Roman road ends go through gate and follow wall on R round to stile in corner, then head L down old green cart-track. Just before reaching beck turn R over stile. ⑪▶ Cross first footbridge. Ignore cattle-grid on L and ford on R. Continue along signposted bridleway. The muddy path eventually gains a surface of stones. Pass to R of farm and along farm road. ⑫▶ Turn L at T-junction, and at end of buildings turn R through gate (FP sign) to follow walled cart-track. ⑬▶ Take RH of two gates, then ignore cart-track to R. Stay by wall on L (FP sign). At end of wall bear L down to stile into wood. Follow main path into wood. ⑭▶ At yellow arrow on tree-trunk turn L to stile, then turn R to follow fence. ⑮▶ Path re-enters wood at small gate. Keep straight on. Just beyond tiny stream turn R (SP Beck Hole) and descend to cross river footbridge. ⑯▶ Turn R along line of disused railway. ⑰▶ Straight on across road. Continue

❗ THE PATH ALONGSIDE WEST BECK HAS SOME ROUGH, ROCKY SECTIONS. NOTHING TOO DIFFICULT, BUT IT'S NOT A PLACE FOR PRAMS AND PUSHCHAIRS.

up The Incline (now grassy) to a gate at the top. Turn R along Beckhole Road to the car park.

GOATHLAND is an attractive and
spacious village where tourists and sheep roam freely all over the place – the latter keeping the wide verges close-cropped. There are some interesting shops, and the North Yorkshire Moors Railway is a star attraction. The War Memorial is a replica of the 7th C Lilla Cross on nearby Fylingdales Moor. The church is of no great antiquity (1896), but is the third church known to have occupied the site since the 12th C. Items of interest include an ancient font (Saxon or early Norman) and a 12th.C altar slab. A diligent search will reveal several mice – the famous trademark of Robert Thompson, the Kilburn wood-carver. Near the church on the Egton Bridge road is the old pinfold where stray animals were kept pending payment of a fine by their owners.

font, Goathland Church

● MALLYAN SPOUT is a minor stream plunging over 70' into West Beck. NELLY AYRE FOSS, a more conventional waterfall, is quite impressive after heavy rain. A descent to stream level here should not be attempted – the bank is slippery and unstable.

● THE ROMAN ROAD ON WHEELDALE MOOR DATES FROM THE 2ND C, AND IS PART OF A ROAD WHICH RAN FROM MALTON (DERVENTIO) TO THE COAST NEAR WHITBY. THIS TREMENDOUS HIGHWAY IS NEARLY 20' WIDE AND STILL HAS ITS ORIGINAL CULVERTS, KERBS AND DITCHES ON EITHER SIDE. WHEN IN USE IT WOULD HAVE HAD A SURFACE OF GRAVEL

Wheeldale Lodge Youth Hostel

● THE INCLINE was constructed in 1836. Carriages and wagons were hauled up and down with water-filled tanks as counterbalances. A steam winding-engine was installed in 1847, but a fatal accident in 1864 led to the incline's closure.

O.S. MAPS : Landranger Series (1 : 50 000) Sheet 94 (Whitby)
Outdoor Leisure 27 (1 : 25 000) NE and SE Sheets

© Jack Keighley 1993

WALKS ON THE
NORTH YORK MOORS

④

BOGGLE HOLE
& RAVENSCAR

5¾ MILES

A magnificent coastal walk presenting spectacular cliff scenery and glorious views across Robin Hood's Bay. The outward route follows the trackbed of the dismantled coastal railway, owned by Scarborough Council and open to the public as an easy and delightful footpath. The walk also offers the opportunity to investigate the old alum quarries and the diverse marine life of the seashore.

Boggle Hole
Youth Hostel
JKeighley

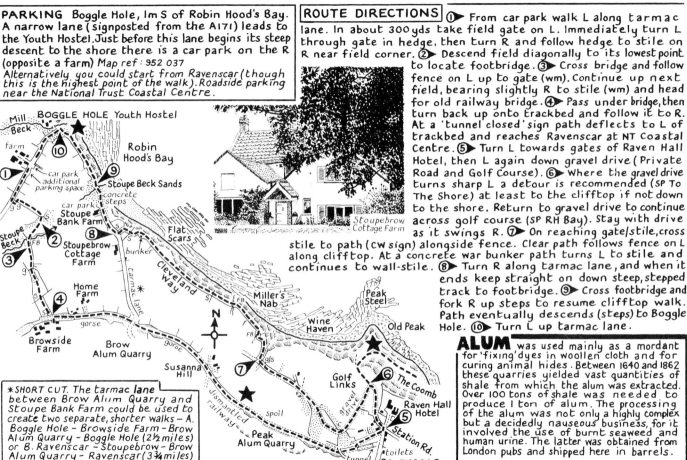

PARKING Boggle Hole, 1m S of Robin Hood's Bay. A narrow lane (signposted from the A171) leads to the Youth Hostel. Just before this lane begins its steep descent to the shore there is a car park on the R (opposite a farm) Map ref: 952 037
Alternatively you could start from Ravenscar (though this is the highest point of the walk). Roadside parking near the National Trust Coastal Centre.

ROUTE DIRECTIONS ① From car park walk L along tarmac lane. In about 300 yds take field gate on L. Immediately turn L through gate in hedge, then turn R and follow hedge to stile on R near field corner. ② Descend field diagonally to its lowest point to locate footbridge. ③ Cross bridge and follow fence on L up to gate (wm). Continue up next field, bearing slightly R to stile (wm) and head for old railway bridge. ④ Pass under bridge, then turn back up onto trackbed and follow it to R. At a 'tunnel closed' sign path deflects to L of trackbed and reaches Ravenscar at NT Coastal Centre. ⑤ Turn L towards gates of Raven Hall Hotel, then L again down gravel drive (Private Road and Golf Course). ⑥ Where the gravel drive turns sharp L a detour is recommended (SP To The Shore) at least to the clifftop if not down to the shore. Return to gravel drive to continue across golf course (SP RH Bay). Stay with drive as it swings R. ⑦ On reaching gate/stile, cross stile to path (CW sign) alongside fence. Clear path follows fence on L along clifftop. At a concrete war bunker path turns L to stile and continues to wall-stile. ⑧ Turn R along tarmac lane, and when it ends keep straight on down steep, stepped track to footbridge. ⑨ Cross footbridge and fork R up steps to resume clifftop walk. Path eventually descends (steps) to Boggle Hole. ⑩ Turn L up tarmac lane.

Stoupebrow Cottage Farm

*SHORT CUT. The tarmac lane between Brow Alum Quarry and Stoupe Bank Farm could be used to create two separate, shorter walks – A. Boggle Hole – Browside Farm – Brow Alum Quarry – Boggle Hole (2½ miles) or B. Ravenscar – Stoupebrow – Brow Alum Quarry – Ravenscar (3¾ miles)

ALUM was used mainly as a mordant for 'fixing' dyes in woollen cloth and for curing animal hides. Between 1640 and 1862 these quarries yielded vast quantities of shale from which the alum was extracted. Over 100 tons of shale was needed to produce 1 ton of alum. The processing of the alum was not only a highly complex but a decidedly nauseous business, for it involved the use of burnt seaweed and human urine. The latter was obtained from London pubs and shipped here in barrels.

BOGGLE HOLE Youth Hostel
Mill Beck
farm
Robin Hood's Bay
⑩
①
car park additional parking space
⑨
Stoupe Beck Sands
concrete steps
car park
Stoupe Bank Farm
⑧
Stoupe Beck
FB
②
Stoupebrow Cottage Farm
③
Flat Scars
bunker
Cleveland Way
Home Farm
④
tarmac lane
Miller's Nab
Peak Steel
Wine Haven
Old Peak
FB
N
Browside Farm
gorse
Brow Alum Quarry
gorse
Susanna Hill
⑦
Golf Links
⑥
The Coomb
Raven Hall Hotel
⑤
Station Rd.
dismantled railway
spoil
Peak Alum Quarry
toilets
tunnel
RAVENSCAR

Sadly the dramatically scenic SCARBOROUGH–WHITBY RAILWAY is no more, for the 'Beeching Axe' fell upon it in 1965. The 21-mile line, engineered by John Waddell, took 13 years to construct and opened in 1885. The tunnel at Ravenscar marked the highest point (631') of the railway.

RAVENSCAR

At the turn of the century there was a grandiose plan afoot to establish a resort here to rival Scarborough. However, 3 major obstacles (instability of land, severe coastal erosion and comparative inaccessibility of beach) eventually caused the project to be abandoned. The sumptuous Raven Hall Hotel was built (as a private residence) in 1774 on the site of a Roman signalling station. A regular guest was George III, who came for treatment during his periodic fits of madness. The building was converted into a luxury hotel in 1889, and was used as a secret military location during World War II.

BOGGLE HOLE YOUTH HOSTEL, AT THE FOOT OF MILL BECK'S WOODED RAVINE, AND ONLY 150 YARDS FROM THE SEA, WAS ORIGINALLY A WATER MILL (BAY MILL). THE PRESENT BUILDING DATES FROM 1837, BUT THERE ARE RECORDS OF A MILL'S EXISTENCE HERE AS FAR BACK AS 1394. THE MILL CLOSED IN 1928 AND THE Y.H.A. BOUGHT THE BUILDING IN 1950. LOCAL FOLKLORE INSISTS THAT THE PLACE IS HAUNTED ('BOGGLE HOLE' DERIVES FROM A BOGGLE, OR GOBLIN, WHO LIVED HERE).

 FOSSILS occur in large numbers all along the Yorkshire coast, and nowhere more so than at Ravenscar. Here are fossils of marine animals of Jurassic vintage (150-185 million years ago). The best examples are often found at the base of the cliffs.

O.S. MAPS : Landranger Series (1:50 000) Sheet 94 (Whitby)
Outdoor Leisure 27 (1:25 000) NE Sheet

© Jack Keighley 1993

 ⑤

ROSEBERRY TOPPING

5 MILES

A steep climb to the delectable rocky summit of the Park's best-known and most instantly recognisable hill, from which coign of vantage one may enjoy extensive views across the Cleveland Plain to the coast. The walk, which is on good paths throughout, extends eastwards over heather moorlands to incorporate, by way of contrast, a peaceful stroll through the forests of Hutton Lowcross.

PARKING Newton under Roseberry, on the A173 Great Ayton - Guisborough road. Sizeable car park at south end of village   Map ref: 570 128

Roseberry Common is crossed by an intricate network of paths. For the sake of clarity, and to avoid confusion (hopefully), only those relevant to the selected route are shown on the map.

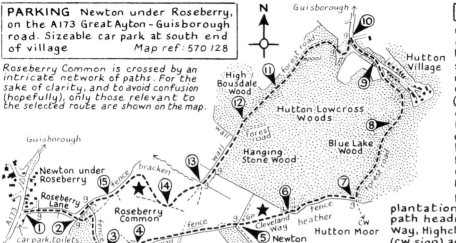

N

Guisborough↑

ROUTE DIRECTIONS ❶ Set off up rough lane which runs alongside village end of car park. ❷ At top of lane go through swing-gate into wood. Keep straight on up broad path, fork L and in a few yards turn sharp R to climb excellent path with wire fence on L. ❸ Turn L through gate to clear path climbing steep upper slope. Path passes to L of summit rocks to reach the O.S. column 'from the back'. ❹ From summit head towards forests on moor to east. Descend steep, slippery slope with care, using zig-zag route where possible, then continue forward along broad path with wall on R. Climb alongside plantation to gate at wall corner. ❺ Take wide path heading ½ L through heather (SP Cleveland Way, Highcliffe Nab). ❻ Go through gate in fence (CW sign) and head R on path between fence and edge of forest. ❼ At junction (where Cleveland Way turns R through gate) turn L down broad, stony forest road. ❽ Cross wide forest road and keep straight on downhill. ❾ Turn L along tarmac road (detour R to visit Hutton Village). ❿ Take small gate on L opposite drive of large house. Turn L along cart-track, which swings R up to gate into wood (short cut straight up field is not a right-of-way). Follow wide forest road. ⑪ At fork keep L (straight on) on rising path. ⑫ When forest road swings L keep straight on along broad path, passing through two gates to reach common. ⑬ Three paths radiate from second gate. Take RH (descending) path. ⑭ Path swings R as it joins another path coming down from L. In 70yds fork R onto good path through bracken. Path gradually curves L to come alongside fence. ⑮ Stay close to fence on R to descend thin path in groove. Re-join outward route at point ② and turn R.

summit of Roseberry Topping

The rocky summit of Roseberry Topping – a dramatic viewpoint – is a grand place to be, though you will be fortunate to have it all to yourself. Don't go too near the crumbling edges of the sheer crags, and keep children under close surveillance.

This renowned peak, though barely exceeding 1000 feet, appears much higher because of its isolation and distinctive conical outline. Geologically the hill is classified as a 'nunatak', which means that during the Ice Age its sandstone summit protruded above the surrounding glaciers. Over the years Roseberry Topping has been quarried for stone, and mined for jet and iron-ore. It was the subsidence caused by ironstone workings coupled with erosion which resulted in the collapse of the west side of the summit in 1912. 1974 saw the birth of the County of Cleveland, and since then the Topping has stood half in the new county and half in North Yorkshire, for the boundary was drawn over its summit. NEWTON WOOD has trees of many species, including sessile oak, rowan, ash, lime, alder and wych-elm. In early summer the wood is carpeted with bluebells and pungent with the smell of ramsons (wild garlic). Roseberry Topping was acquired by the N.T. in 1985.

Ramsons

HUTTON VILLAGE is mostly modern houses - the homes of commuters.

The village's most notable feature is its forest setting.

HEATHER

The North York Moors National Park is famous for its vast expanses of heather moorland, and NEWTON MOOR and HUTTON MOOR are fine examples. Three different types of heather may be found. LING (Calluna vulgaris) is the most common, turning the moors purple in August ('Calluna' is from the Greek 'Kallino'-to beautify or adorn). BELL HEATHER (Erica cinerea) has larger and usually paler flowers than ling. The beautiful CROSS-LEAVED HEATH (Erica tetralix) grows in boggy areas. The rose-pink flowers are egg-shaped, and the leaves are arranged in fours.

Bell Heather

Cross-leaved Heath

O.S. MAPS : Landranger Series (1 : 50 000) Sheet 93 (Middlesbrough and Darlington). Outdoor Leisure 26 (1 : 25 000) NW Sheet

© Jack Keighley 1993

23

---

(6)

BRANSDALE

7½ MILES

The head of Bransdale is one of the remotest places in the North York Moors. The first and last sections of this grand walk, through, respectively, riverside pastures and coniferous forest, contrast strikingly with the wild splendour of the heather moors. It should be noted that 4½ miles of the route is across moorland which offers no vestige of shelter in bad weather.

Cockayne Church

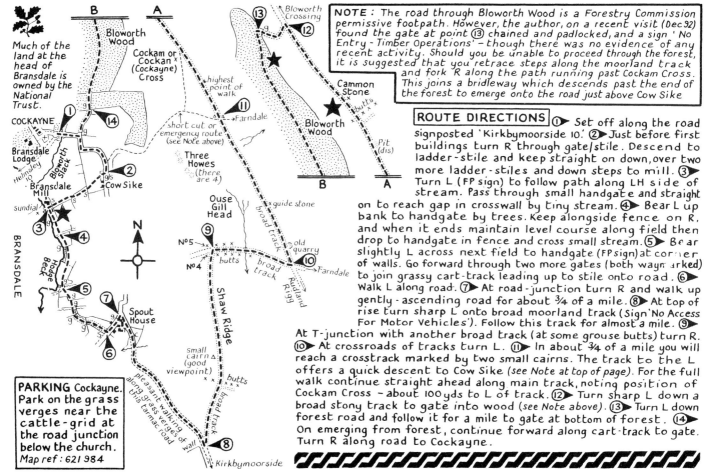

Much of the land at the head of Bransdale is owned by the National Trust.

NOTE: The road through Bloworth Wood is a Forestry Commission permissive footpath. However, the author, on a recent visit (Dec 92) found the gate at point (13) chained and padlocked, and a sign 'No Entry - Timber Operations' - though there was no evidence of any recent activity. Should you be unable to proceed through the forest, it is suggested that you retrace steps along the moorland track and fork R along the path running past Cockam Cross. This joins a bridleway which descends past the end of the forest to emerge onto the road just above Cow Sike

ROUTE DIRECTIONS (1) Set off along the road signposted 'Kirkbymoorside 10'. (2) Just before first buildings turn R through gate/stile. Descend to ladder-stile and keep straight on down, over two more ladder-stiles and down steps to mill. (3) Turn L (FP sign) to follow path along LH side of stream. Pass through small handgate and straight on to reach gap in crosswall by tiny stream. (4) Bear L up bank to handgate by trees. Keep alongside fence on R, and when it ends maintain level course along field then drop to handgate in fence and cross small stream. (5) Bear slightly L across next field to handgate (FP sign) at corner of walls. Go forward through two more gates (both waymarked) to join grassy cart-track leading up to stile onto road. (6) Walk L along road. (7) At road-junction turn R and walk up gently-ascending road for about ¾ of a mile. (8) At top of rise turn sharp L onto broad moorland track (Sign'No Access For Motor Vehicles'). Follow this track for almost a mile. (9) At T-junction with another broad track (at some grouse butts) turn R. (10) At crossroads of tracks turn L. (11) In about ¾ of a mile you will reach a crosstrack marked by two small cairns. The track to the L offers a quick descent to Cow Sike (see Note at top of page). For the full walk continue straight ahead along main track, noting position of Cockam Cross - about 100 yds to L of track. (12) Turn sharp L down a broad stony track to gate into wood (see Note above). (13) Turn L down forest road and follow it for a mile to gate at bottom of forest. (14) On emerging from forest, continue forward along cart-track to gate. Turn R along road to Cockayne.

PARKING Cockayne. Park on the grass verges near the cattle-grid at the road junction below the church. Map ref: 621 984

24

The lonely settlement of COCKAYNE is barely large enough to be classed even as a hamlet, but is worth a visit on account of its tiny CHURCH OF ST. NICHOLAS. It is suggested that a detour be made to this little gem *before* starting the walk; if left until the end, tired legs may object to the steep climb. You could, however, take the car up - there is a small parking space at the sharp bend just past the church. The building replaced the old Cockan Chapel in 1886 on a site where a church has stood since medieval times. Of particular interest is the unusual barrelled ceiling over the nave and chancel.

BRANSDALE MILL

The small mill which had stood here since Norman times was developed into a small industrial complex by William Strickland from 1811 onwards. The various inscriptions, in Hebrew, Greek and Latin, which adorn the buildings are the work of Strickland's son Emmanuel, a former vicar of Ingleby Greenhow. The mill closed down in 1935, and was acquired by the National Trust in 1968. Across the bridge, and somewhat incongruously sited in the middle of a field, is a large, pedestal-type sundial.

sundial, Bransdale Mill

Cockam Cross

Cammon Stone. Inscribed 'Hallelujah' - in Hebrew. (Emmanuel Strickland was here)

O.S. MAPS : Landranger Series (1:50 000) Sheet 94 (Whitby)
Outdoor Leisure 26 (1:25 000) SW and NW Sheets

(7)

RIEVAULX ABBEY & OLD BYLAND

6 MILES

A popular walk, and understandably so, for its numerous highlights include a ruin of stunning grandeur, lovely old bridges, fine woodland and valley scenery and a sleepy old village with a little gem of a church. An ideal ramble for a frosty winter's day, when normally muddy sections will be hard-frozen - and you *may* have the abbey almost to yourself!

All Saints' Church, Old Byland

PARKING The car park at Rievaulx Abbey is specifically for the use of abbey visitors. The best parking place is ¾ of a mile from Rievaulx Bridge along the Scawton road. A track emerges from the corner of the forest at a gate marked with a white acorn sign and a notice – 'Private Road - No Admittance to Vehicles'. There is space to park several cars here without blocking access.
Map ref : 563 845

ROUTE DIRECTIONS ① ▶ Walk down road (SP Cleveland Way, Rievaulx 1 mile). Ignore road branching L past Ashberry Farm. ② ▶ Cross Rievaulx Bridge, turn L and follow road to Abbey. ③ ▶ After visiting Abbey, continue along road towards Rievaulx village. ④ ▶ After second building on L turn L through gate (Footpath to Bow Bridge). Pass through gate to L of stables and go forward across small stream to gate (wm). Keep straight on through kissing-gate (wm) and alongside fence on R to reach two fence-stiles near river. ⑤ ▶ Cross these, then follow river upstream for about 100 yds before turning R (wm) up to stile. Turn L along rough lane and follow it over Bow Bridge. ⑥ ▶ Go through gate/stile on R (Footpath to Hawnby) and along path close to fence on R. Beyond next stile a wooden walkway is followed. At end of walkway keep straight on across field to gate/stile at far LH corner. ⑦ ▶ Turn R up farm road. ⑧ ▶ Where road turns R down to farm turn sharp L up cart-track. ⑨ ▶ When cart-track turns L leave it in favour of stile on R (SP Old Byland). Follow fence on R through three stiles, and at corner of next field turn L (SP Old Byland). Follow hedge on R to reach ladder-stile onto road. ⑩ ▶ Turn R and first L to follow road through village (church is on L across green). Road curves R. Keep straight on at junction of roads. ⑪ ▶ 50 yds past village name sign go through small gate on L and descend L. Clear path crosses floor of valley, climbs through trees and runs close to wall on R. ⑫ ▶ Go through gate in wall and up to gate behind telegraph pole. Walk along LH edge of two fields to small gate (wm) into wood. ⑬ ▶ Descend path to L, go over footbridge. ⑭ ▶ Cross narrow field to stile. Beyond it you will see two footbridges to your L. Ignore the first. Cross the second and turn L along forest road.

path may be blocked here by low wire netting which will have to be stridden (strided? strode?)

Tylas Farm
Tylas Barn
Oxen Dale
mud
muddy field
farm road
wooden walkway
OLD BYLAND
All Saints'
Old Byland Hall
Hill Gill
track
fence
Lambert Hag Wood
Bow Bridge
remains of Canal
former mill
Rievaulx
R. Rye
wall
hedge
Callister Wood
● Still visible between Rievaulx and the R.Rye is the course of a canal built in the 12th.C. It provided a water supply for the monks, and was also used to ferry stone for building the abbey. ● The small lakes in Nettle Dale were once abbey fishponds.
Nettle Dale
Nature Reserve - private
FB
FB
forest road
RIEVAULX ABBEY
car park, toilets
charming cottage
Rievaulx Terrace
Old Byland
Ashberry Farm
Scawton
Hagg Hall
Rievaulx Bridge
Helmsley 3

RIEVAULX BRIDGE was built to replace its medieval predecessor which was destroyed by floods in 1754. The original BOW BRIDGE was swept away by the same floods, and its replacement was designed by JOHN CARR, an eminent 18thC architect whose work includes Harewood House (near Leeds).

N

Ashberry Farm

RIEVAULX ABBEY

Founded in 1131 by a colony of 13 monks from Clairvaulx, Rievaulx, ('valley of the Rye'), was the first large Cistercian church to be built in northern England. Construction took more than a century, and, because of the westward slope of the site, the church is on a NW-SE axis instead of the customary W-E. Under its third abbot, Ailred (1147-67), Rievaulx reached the zenith of its prosperity. At this time there were over 140 monks and nearly 500 lay brothers in residence, and the abbey owned some 14,000 sheep, besides being involved in mining, fishing, agriculture and tanning. Thereafter the abbey went into debt and decline, and at the Dissolution (1538) only 22 monks remained. The last abbot,

dawn at Rievaulx

Sedburgh, was hanged for his alleged involvement in the Pilgrimage of Grace. Fountains and Rievaulx are Yorkshire's finest ecclesiastical ruins. Fountains is more complete, and more beautiful in its entire setting, but for the stunning grandeur of its church architecture Rievaulx is incomparable. OPEN : 29 Mar - 30 Sep Daily 10-6 ; 1 Oct - 29 Mar Tue to Sun 10-4.

TYLAS

was the site chosen by monks from Hood Grange (*see Walk 30*) who came here in 1143 to build a new abbey. For four years they laboured at their task, but the close proximity to the already well-established Rievaulx caused various problems, and in 1147 the newcomers packed their bags and departed to a site near Oldstead. They remained there for 30 years before moving once more - this time to Byland.

St. Ailred - Rievaulx's greatest abbot

DON'T PASS THROUGH OLD BYLAND WITHOUT VISITING THE LITTLE 12TH C. CHURCH. NOTE THE UPSIDE-DOWN SUNDIAL (E. WALL OF TOWER)

O.S. MAPS : Landranger Series (1:50 000) Sheet 100 (Malton and Pickering).   Outdoor Leisure 26 (1:25 000) SW Sheet

© Jack Keighley 1993

KEPWICK & THE DROVE ROAD

5¾ MILES

Of the many ancient highways in the North York Moors, the most famous is the Hambleton Drove Road, a classic green track undulating along the high moors above the region's abrupt western escarpment. All walks around this escarpment are beautiful, and this is one of the best, for the climb from the pretty village of Kepwick is a sheer delight.

J Keighley   *Kepwick Church*

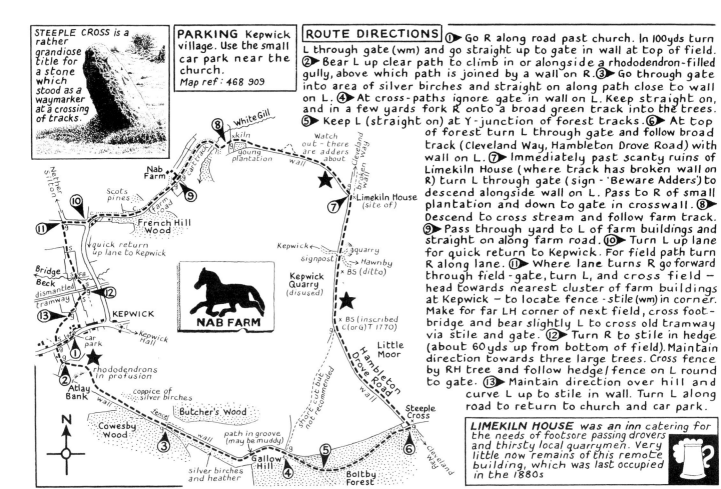

STEEPLE CROSS is a rather grandiose title for a stone which stood as a waymarker at a crossing of tracks.

PARKING Kepwick village. Use the small car park near the church. Map ref: 468 909

ROUTE DIRECTIONS

① Go R along road past church. In 100yds turn L through gate (wm) and go straight up to gate in wall at top of field. ② Bear L up clear path to climb in or alongside a rhododendron-filled gully, above which path is joined by a wall on R. ③ Go through gate into area of silver birches and straight on along path close to wall on L. ④ At cross-paths ignore gate in wall on L. Keep straight on, and in a few yards fork R onto a broad green track into the trees. ⑤ Keep L (straight on) at Y-junction of forest tracks. ⑥ At top of forest turn L through gate and follow broad track (Cleveland Way, Hambleton Drove Road) with wall on L. ⑦ Immediately past scanty ruins of Limekiln House (where track has broken wall on R) turn L through gate (sign - 'Beware Adders') to descend alongside wall on L. Pass to R of small plantation and down to gate in crosswall. ⑧ Descend to cross stream and follow farm track. ⑨ Pass through yard to L of farm buildings and straight on along farm road. ⑩ Turn L up lane for quick return to Kepwick. For field path turn R along lane. ⑪ Where lane turns R go forward through field-gate, turn L, and cross field — head towards nearest cluster of farm buildings at Kepwick — to locate fence-stile (wm) in corner. Make for far LH corner of next field, cross footbridge and bear slightly L to cross old tramway via stile and gate. ⑫ Turn R to stile in hedge (about 60 yds up from bottom of field). Maintain direction towards three large trees. Cross fence by RH tree and follow hedge/fence on L round to gate. ⑬ Maintain direction over hill and curve L up to stile in wall. Turn L along road to return to church and car park.

LIMEKILN HOUSE was an inn catering for the needs of footsore passing drovers and thirsty local quarrymen. Very little now remains of this remote building, which was last occupied in the 1880s

White Gill

kiln

young plantation

Watch out - there are adders about

Cleveland Way

broken wall

wall

Nab Farm

car track

farm road

Scots pines

French Hill Wood

Limekiln House (site of)

Nether Silton

quick return up lane to Kepwick

Kepwick signpost

quarry

Hawnby

BS (ditto)

Kepwick Quarry (disused)

Bridge Beck

dismantled tramway

KEPWICK

Kepwick Hall

car park

BS (inscribed C (or G) T 1770)

Little Moor

Hambleton Drove Road

wall

NAB FARM

rhododendrons in profusion

Atlay Bank

coppice of silver birches

Butcher's Wood

path in groove (may be muddy)

Cowesby Wood

wall

fence

Gallow Hill

silver birches and heather

Boltby Forest

short-cut but not recommended

Steeple Cross

Cleveland Way

N

THE HAMBLETON DROVE ROAD

In pre-refrigeration days meat had to be eaten soon after slaughter, and therefore had to be moved to its place of consumption whilst it was still alive. Vast droves of cattle and sheep were taken incredible distances along upland routes designed to avoid the costly turnpike roads. Such a route ran from Scotland to the south and east of England, passing over the Hambleton Hills between Swainby and Oldstead. This 15-mile section is known as the Hambleton Drove Road. Droving reached its peak during the 18th C. Industrial Revolution, when the hardy drovers and their dogs would manoeuvre herds of up to 200 head of cattle or sheep. Pigs, geese, turkeys and packhorses were also taken along the drove roads.

BEWARE ADDERS

Of the three snakes found in Britain only the adder (vipera berus) is venomous. It rarely exceeds 20" in length, and, though individuals vary greatly in colour, is instantly recognisable by its dark zig-zag markings. Two further distinguishing features are the V-mark behind the head and the red eyes with slit-like pupils. Adders pose no great threat to humans; when disturbed they glide away in search of cover, and will not bite unless provoked. They hibernate from November to March, and are most commonly seen in early summer on dry, south-facing slopes, where they like to bask in the sunshine. Their prey consists mainly of lizards, frogs and small mammals (one good meal will suffice for a week or so). Adders are decreasing in number, and are protected under the Wildlife and Countryside Act.

O.S. MAPS : Landranger Series (1:50 000) Sheet 100 (Malton and Pickering)   Outdoor Leisure 26 (1:25 000) SW Sheet

© Jack Keighley 1993

LASTINGHAM & SPAUNTON MOOR

8 MILES

Nestling cosily in a pretty hollow on the ridge between Farndale and Rosedale is the beautiful and historic village of Lastingham. Its far-famed Parish Church is absolutely superb, and should not be missed; nor should the walk here described – an invigorating hike over wild moorland followed by a delectable return along the colourful Seven valley.

The Crypt, Lastingham

J Keighley

29

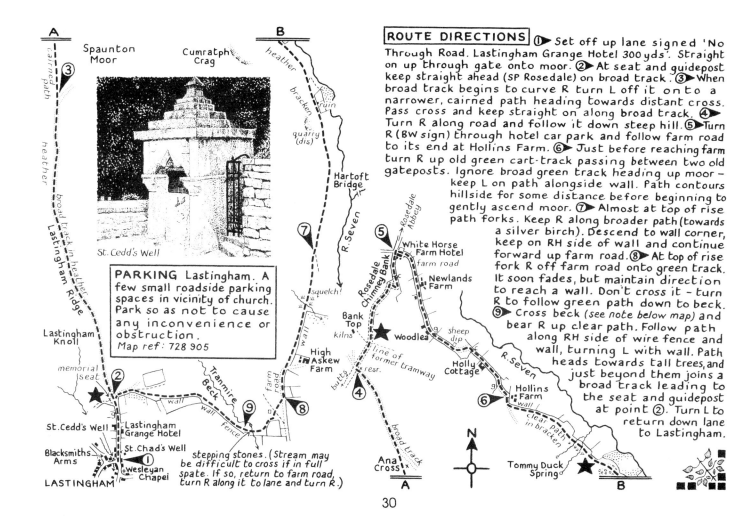

Spaunton Moor

Cumratph Crag

③

St. Cedd's Well

PARKING Lastingham. A few small roadside parking spaces in vicinity of church. Park so as not to cause any inconvenience or obstruction.
Map ref: 728 905

heather

bracken

ruin

quarry (dis)

Hartoft Bridge

R. Seven

⑦

squelch!

cairned path

broad track in heather

Lastingham Ridge

heather

Lastingham Knoll

memorial seat

②

St.Cedd's Well

Lastingham Grange Hotel

St.Chad's Well

Blacksmiths Arms

①

Wesleyan Chapel

LASTINGHAM

Tranmire Beck

wall

wall fence

⑨

farm road

High Askew Farm

⑧

wall

kilns

Bank Top

butts

resr.

Line of former tramway

④

Woodlea

★

stepping stones. (Stream may be difficult to cross if in full spate. If so, return to farm road, turn R along it to lane and turn R.)

Ana Cross

broad track

Rosedale Abbey

⑤

White Horse Farm Hotel

farm road

Rosedale Chimney Bank

Newlands Farm

sheep dip

Holly Cottage

R. Seven

⑥

Hollins Farm

wall

clear path in bracken

Tommy Duck Spring

★

N

ROUTE DIRECTIONS ① Set off up lane signed 'No Through Road. Lastingham Grange Hotel 300 yds'. Straight on up through gate onto moor. ② At seat and guidepost keep straight ahead (SP Rosedale) on broad track. ③ When broad track begins to curve R turn L off it onto a narrower, cairned path heading towards distant cross. Pass cross and keep straight on along broad track. ④ Turn R along road and follow it down steep hill. ⑤ Turn R (BW sign) through hotel car park and follow farm road to its end at Hollins Farm. ⑥ Just before reaching farm turn R up old green cart-track passing between two old gateposts. Ignore broad green track heading up moor – keep L on path alongside wall. Path contours hillside for some distance before beginning to gently ascend moor. ⑦ Almost at top of rise path forks. Keep R along broader path (towards a silver birch). Descend to wall corner, keep on RH side of wall and continue forward up farm road. ⑧ At top of rise fork R off farm road onto green track. It soon fades, but maintain direction to reach a wall. Don't cross it – turn R to follow green path down to beck. ⑨ Cross beck (see note below map) and bear R up clear path. Follow path along RH side of wire fence and wall, turning L with wall. Path heads towards tall trees, and just beyond them joins a broad track leading to the seat and guidepost at point ②. Turn L to return down lane to Lastingham.

Blacksmiths Arms

LASTINGHAM

, one of the most delightful villages in the National Park, is an ancient cradle of Christianity. Cedd, a Lindisfarne monk, came this way and initiated the building of a monastery in 654. Following his death, from plague, in 664, the task was completed by his brother Chad, but the wooden structure was destroyed by the Danes. In 1078 Stephen of Whitby began to erect a stone abbey on the Celtic foundations, but ten years later, before the work was finished, the Benedictine monks moved to York. Beneath the Parish Church, which now occupies the site, lies one of Britain's finest examples of 11th.C architecture — a superb Norman crypt which dates from c1078. The magnificent vaulted stone roof of the church copies the pattern of that in the crypt, and was constructed in 1879. The cosy pub (Blacksmiths Arms) opposite the church is also the village Post Office.

The tall shaft of ANA (Ainhowe or One Howe) CROSS is a modern replacement. Remains of the ancient original shaft can be seen in The Crypt.

ROSEDALE CHIMNEY BANK is one of Britain's steepest motor roads (max.gradient 1 in 3). It is named after a 100' engine-house chimney which once stood at the Bank Top (it was demolished July 1972). Here was the southern terminus of the Ironstone Railway (1861-1929). Plainly visible is a row of kilns which roasted the iron-ore to expel water and carbonic acid gas. Lovely views from here of Rosedale.

NOTE : SECTIONS ③-④ AND ⑨-⑫ ARE NOT OFFICIAL RIGHTS-OF-WAY. THEY ARE, HOWEVER, MUCH-USED BY WALKERS, AND YOU SHOULDN'T ENCOUNTER ANY PROBLEMS

O.S.MAPS: Landranger Series (1:50 000) Sheet 100 (Malton, Pickering)
Outdoor Leisure 26 (1:25 000) SW Sheet and 27 SE Sheet

A BIRD'S-EYE VIEW OF GUISBOROUGH

7 MILES

The historic market town of Guisborough nestles cosily in the lee of the steep escarpment on its south side. It is around these wooded slopes that our walk progresses, meandering along forest tracks to reach a dramatic climax at Highcliff Nab. Of the many fine viewpoints mentioned within these pages, this jutting rocky knoll is the most spectacular.

Gisborough Priory

JKeighley

31

PARKING Guisborough. Large car park just off the A171 Whitby Road at the eastern end of the town. Map ref: 615 158

ROUTE DIRECTIONS ① Leave car park at telephone kiosk, turn R, then L at T-junction and R at lights to church and priory. ② Pass along L side of church and along paved path. When path turns L go ½ R through metal swing-gate and follow tarmac path across fields to A171. ③ Turn L along road, then R over cattle-grid onto farm road (SP Foxdale Farm Only). ④ Go L through stile (FP sign) near fence corner. Walk forward with fence on R to metal swing-gate and keep straight on with fence on L to stile. ⑤ Pass along path between hedges and straight on along obvious path through three more stiles.

⑥ Just before reaching A171 turn sharp R up farm road. Cross line of old railway and keep straight ahead along farm road. ⑦ Fork L over cattle-grid and up broad track. ⑧ Turn R over stile (CW sign) and follow fence on L. Cross tiny ravine, turn R over stile and L (cw) along grass track at edge of wood. ⑨ Ignore wm footpath to R, but a little further on turn R (CW sign) along broad track with wall on R. Keep straight on along main track, which eventually descends to T-junction. ⑩ Turn L on wide grass track. ⑪ Fork L up rising path, then head R along forest road. ⑫ Where forest road bends L, turn R along clear path to Highcliff Nab. ⑬ Turn L at summit to descend path which curves R to foot of crags, where take second turning on L to descend steep firebreak. Cross forest road and continue straight down to bottom of forest. ⑭ Turn sharp R to follow track along edge of forest. ⑮ Turn L onto path between spoil heaps. It soon rejoins main track. ⑯ At crossroads of tracks go straight forward (leaving main track). Pass very long building, leave wood at stile and continue forward on green path through gorse to reach gate (wm). ⑰ Turn R through gate into wood and immediately L onto narrow path by fence. (Ignore the broad forest tracks). Keep close to fence on L at edge of forest. ⑱ Turn L down rough track between hedges. Follow it to A171 and turn L to follow main road back into Guisborough.

GUISBOROUGH

② Grammar School

this is not a spelling mistake

Gisborough Hall

⑥

Priory

tarmac path

A171 Whitby

disused railway

A171 Middlesbrough

A171 Whitby

① car park, toilets, information

③

④

⑤

⑦ concrete

CW

Foxdale Farm

Old Park Farm

⑧

N

disused railway

Butt Lane

⑨

⑰

⑱

gorse

Belman Bank Guisborough Woods

housing estate

⑭

stables

⑯

⑩

Kemplah Wood

⑮

muddy descent

Highcliff Wood

ignore green path branching L

forest road

⑪

Highcliff Nab

wide forest road

⑬ ⑫

THE CLEVELAND ESCARPMENT has many spoil heaps left from old mining operations. BELMAN BANK was the site of Britain's first alum mine (c1595)

WHITBY 21 GUISBOROUGH 1

32

GUISBOROUGH AND ITS PRIORY

Though now largely a 'dormitory' town for industrial Teesside, Guisborough, one-time capital of Cleveland, still retains much of its ancient market-town character. Its focal point is the old market cross, adorned with sundial and standing at the eastern end of a wide main street lined with cobbles and attractive shops. Beyond the cross to the east is the fine Parish Church of St. Nicholas, which, though substantially rebuilt 1903-8, still displays portions of wall dating from around 1500 in its chancel and tower. Visitors will find much of interest, notably some medieval mosaic floor tiles from the Priory and the intriguing de Brus Cenotaph (c1520), which links the local Bruce family to the Scottish King Robert the Bruce.

An Augustinian canon

THE AUGUSTINIAN PRIORY was founded c1119

Of what was one of the richest houses in the land little remains save for the magnificent 13th C east wall of the church, which is complete except for the tracery of its 56' high window. The church, which was destroyed by fire in 1289 and rebuilt, was 352' long and 97' high.

Map labels: Gatehouse · N. Transept · modern boundary wall · Nave · Tower · Choir · Presbytery · Cloister Garth · Cellarer's Range · S. Transept · Dormitory Range · Refectory · Service Passage · Kitchen

It is said that the ghost of a black monk visits the ruins once a year at midnight on the first new moon.

HIGHCLIFF NAB
is a craggy gritstone outcrop. From its top (981') there is a marvellous view of Guisborough. Beyond is the industrial sprawl of Teesside. The tip of Roseberry Topping is just visible to the west.

O.S. MAPS : Landranger Series (1:50,000) Sheet 94 (Whitby)
Outdoor Leisure 26 (1:25 000) NW Sheet

© Jack Keighley 1993

---

(11)

A TRIP INTO THORODALE

5¾ MILES

The peaceful little church at Hawnby, in its idyllic riverside setting, makes a perfect starting-point for an exploration of the little-known valley of Thorodale. The wide diversity of terrain – upland pasture, open moor, riverbank and woodland – provides a walk of sustained interest and ever-changing scenery. Nowhere in the North York Moors will you find countryside lovelier than this.

Arden Hall
Thorodale

J Keighley

PARKING Dalicar Bridge (footbridge) near Hawnby Church, ½ mile W of the village by the Kepwick road. Parking space on roadside verge between church and bridge.
Map ref: 538 897

ROUTE DIRECTIONS ① Cross footbridge and turn R alongside river. ② Bear L above small bank of trees, and in 70yds bear R (wm) up clear path to stile by gate. Straight on up, steeply, and on reaching fence keep to R of it (wm). ③ Turn L over stile (wm). ④ Just before reaching large barn turn R up to guidepost and R again (SP Dale Town Common) along cart-track which climbs to come alongside a wood. ⑤ When cart-track forks keep L on upper track. Pass to L of some barns and straight on to reach a gate onto open moor. ⑥ Turn R on broad green track which eventually bears L away from wall and down to gate in crosswall. Follow track over next hill. ⑦ Turn R down rough lane (the old Hawnby - Kepwick road). ⑧ Turn L down drive to Arden Hall, L again at bottom and R at far side of row of cottages (BW sign). Follow cart-track down over stream and up through wood. ⑨ When cart-track bears L go up to gate on R. Follow RH field-boundary. ⑩ Turn L up farm road, R through farmyard and straight on along farm road. ⑪ When farm road turns L take stile on R and follow fence to a gate into wood. Follow broad track along edge of wood. ⑫ Cross stream (FB/ford) and take gate on L. Re-cross stream at another footbridge. Keep on down to river, where turn L through gate and head upstream to cross big footbridge. ⑬ Thin path heads L upstream, but soon swings R to climb to gate at edge of wood. Don't use this gate; instead turn R to follow thin path which maintains a fairly level course to another edge-of-wood gate. ⑭ Follow old cart-track, which passes directly in front of Carr House. In next field, cart-track turns down R towards wood. ⑮ Leave track at this point and go straight on past isolated gate (wm). Continue along LH side of wood to eventually join a cart-track leading down to road. Turn R down to church.

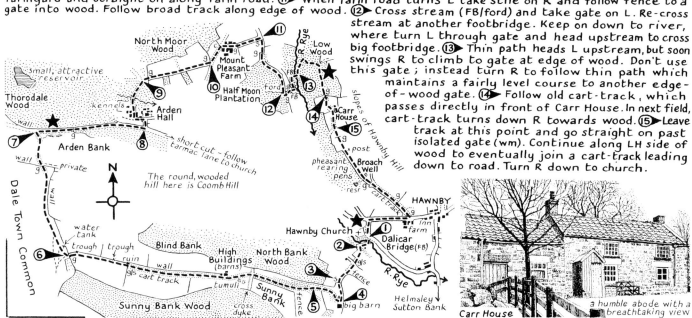

a humble abode with a breathtaking view

Carr House

34

All Saints', Hawnby

This lovely little church stands isolated from the village in a tranquil wooded setting on the banks of the infant Rye. The building was extensively restored in Victorian times, but dates back to the Normans, and evidence of 14th C. repair work suggests that the church may have been damaged by raiding Scots. An unusual piece of stained glass in the west window depicts army stretcher-bearers attending to a wounded soldier, and nearby a framed extract from the Yorkshire Herald of 23-10-1916 tells of the proud war record of the parish. Also remembered are 4 German airmen of 7 Squadron Luftwaffe who died in action over Hawnby 17-12-1942.

ARDEN HALL

An impressive, though architecturally somewhat severe, mansion which stands on the site of the former Arden Priory, a Benedictine nunnery dedicated to St. Andrew. Arden Hall, for centuries the home of the Tancred family, is the seat of the Earls of Mexborough. It is said that Mary, Queen of Scots, once slept here (where *didn't* she?). The house has extensive and elaborate gardens, and the surrounding woods produce colourful displays of spring flowers.

Look out for HARES between High Buildings and Dale Town Common, where the rolling upland pastures flanked by woodland provide an ideal habitat. The brown hare is a creature much given to eccentric behaviour (hence the expression 'hare-brained'), particularly so in March, when the jacks (males) will leap, kick and stand on hind legs to box with each other in a ritual designed to impress the does prior to mating.

O.S. MAPS : Landranger Series (1:50 000) Sheet 100 (Malton and Pickering)   Outdoor Leisure 26 (1:25 000) SW Sheet

(12)

LOWER GLAISDALE

7 MILES

The ancient and graceful Beggar's Bridge, a famed tourist attraction, is the starting-point of this varied and scenic perambulation. 'Lower Glaisdale' makes a convenient title, though the walk strays into the small, neighbouring valley of Butter Beck in order to incorporate 'Packman's Trod' – a paved path winding through glorious woodland high above one of the Esk's most spectacular gorges.

Beggar's Bridge

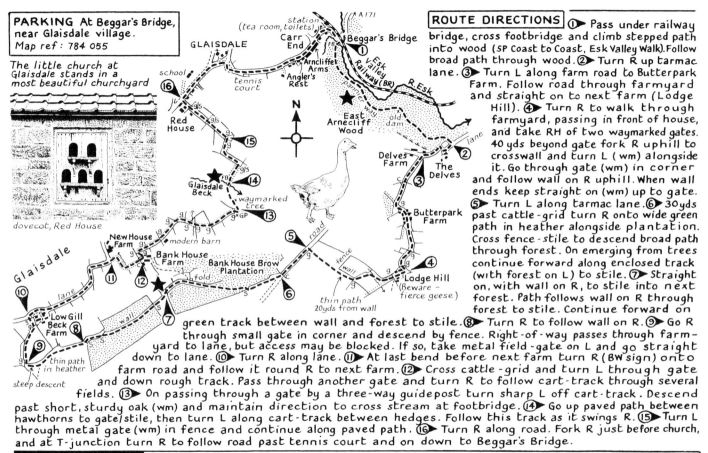

PARKING At Beggar's Bridge, near Glaisdale village.
Map ref: 784 055

The little church at Glaisdale stands in a most beautiful churchyard

dovecot, Red House

① Pass under railway bridge, cross footbridge and climb stepped path into wood (SP Coast to Coast, Esk Valley Walk). Follow broad path through wood. **②** Turn R up tarmac lane. **③** Turn L along farm road to Butterpark Farm. Follow road through farmyard and straight on to next farm (Lodge Hill). **④** Turn R to walk through farmyard, passing in front of house, and take RH of two waymarked gates. 40 yds beyond gate fork R uphill to crosswall and turn L (wm) alongside it. Go through gate (wm) in corner and follow wall on R uphill. When wall ends keep straight on (wm) up to gate. **⑤** Turn L along tarmac lane. **⑥** 30 yds past cattle-grid turn R onto wide green path in heather alongside plantation. Cross fence-stile to descend broad path through forest. On emerging from trees continue forward along enclosed track (with forest on L) to stile. **⑦** Straight on, with wall on R, to stile into next forest. Path follows wall on R through forest to stile. Continue forward on green track between wall and forest to stile. **⑧** Turn R to follow wall on R. **⑨** Go R through small gate in corner and descend by fence. Right-of-way passes through farmyard to lane, but access may be blocked. If so, take metal field-gate on L and go straight down to lane. **⑩** Turn R along lane. **⑪** At last bend before next farm turn R (BW sign) onto farm road and follow it round R to next farm. **⑫** Cross cattle-grid and turn L through gate and down rough track. Pass through another gate and turn R to follow cart-track through several fields. **⑬** On passing through a gate by a three-way guidepost turn sharp L off cart-track. Descend past short, sturdy oak (wm) and maintain direction to cross stream at footbridge. **⑭** Go up paved path between hawthorns to gate/stile, then turn L along cart-track between hedges. Follow this track as it swings R. **⑮** Turn L through metal gate (wm) in fence and continue along paved path. **⑯** Turn R along road. Fork R just before church, and at T-junction turn R to follow road past tennis court and on down to Beggar's Bridge.

GLAISDALE

A peaceful, pastoral valley now, Glaisdale would have presented a very different picture during the iron-mining boom of the 1800s. Mining ceased in 1876, but numerous vestiges of former industry still remain.

THE STORY OF Beggar's Bridge

Tom Ferries, the son of a poor sheep farmer, met and fell in love with Agnes Richardson, daughter of a wealthy Glaisdale landowner. Her father was aghast at the prospect of Agnes marrying a 'beggar', but consented to allow the wedding if and when Tom became a rich man. Tom went to sea in 1586, took part in the defeat of the Armada and sailed, subsequently, with Sir Francis Drake to the West Indies, where he grew rich through piracy. He returned to England, and married Agnes, in 1592. The couple settled in Hull, where Ferries became City Sheriff and, later, Lord Mayor. Agnes died in 1618 and the following year Tom, mindful of the difficulties he had had as a youth in crossing the Esk to meet her, and of her father's hostility, commissioned 'Beggar's Bridge' to be built as a memorial.

Packman's Trod

PANNIER WAYS like the one through East Arncliff Wood are common in the North York Moors and date from the late 16th C. onwards. The blocks, their surfaces now hollowed by the passage of hooves and feet, were placed to facilitate the movement of teams of ponies laden with panniers carrying cloth, coal, lime, ironstone etc.

Delves Farm

GLAISDALE RAILWAY STATION opened in 1865 and was originally called *Beggar's Bridge Station*.

O.S. MAPS : Landranger Series (1 : 50 000) Sheet 94 (Whitby) Outdoor Leisure 27 (1 : 25 000) NE Sheet

© Jack Keighley 1993

WHISPER DALES

6¾ MILES

The 'Fairyland' image induced by this evocative and romantic-sounding name is not inappropriate, for Whisper Dales - a secret valley enclosed by shapely, wooded hills - is a place of quite magical beauty. The panoramic view from Reasty Bank, the floriferous Hilda Wood and the lovely church at Hackness are additional highlights of this splendid walk.

Whisper Dales

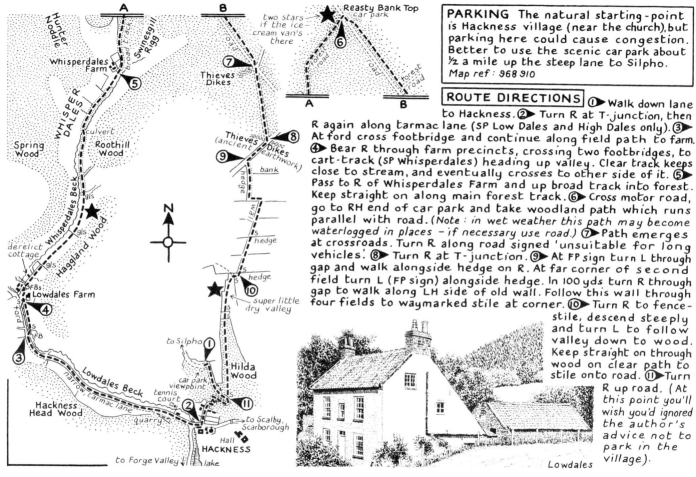

Map labels:

A

B

Reasty Bank Top
car park

two stars
if the ice-
cream van's
there

⑥

Nidd Hunter Moor

Swinesgill Rigg

broad track

Whisperdales
Farm

⑤

⑦

Thieves
Dikes

road

forest road

forest road

forest road

A

B

WHISPER DALES

Spring
Wood

Roothill
Wood

culvert

Thieves
(ancient
Dikes
earthwork)

⑧

⑨

bank

hedge

Whisperdales Beck

gls

N

gls

Haggland Wood

wall

s

hedge

gls

derelict
cottage

gls

s

hedge

⑩

super little
dry valley

BFBs

Lowdales Farm

s

④

s

FB

③

to Silpho

①

s

Hilda
Wood

Lowdales Beck

car park
viewpoint

②

⑪

narrow tarmac lane

tennis
court

to Scalby,
Scarborough

Hackness
Head Wood

quarry

Hall
HACKNESS

to Forge Valley

lake

PARKING The natural starting-point
is Hackness village (near the church), but
parking here could cause congestion.
Better to use the scenic car park about
½ a mile up the steep lane to Silpho.
Map ref: 968 910

ROUTE DIRECTIONS ① Walk down lane
to Hackness. ② Turn R at T-junction, then
R again along tarmac lane (SP Low Dales and High Dales only). ③
At ford cross footbridge and continue along field path to farm.
④ Bear R through farm precincts, crossing two footbridges, to
cart-track (SP Whisperdales) heading up valley. Clear track keeps
close to stream, and eventually crosses to other side of it. ⑤
Pass to R of Whisperdales Farm and up broad track into forest.
Keep straight on along main forest track. ⑥ Cross motor road,
go to RH end of car park and take woodland path which runs
parallel with road. (Note: in wet weather this path may become
waterlogged in places - if necessary use road.) ⑦ Path emerges
at crossroads. Turn R along road signed 'unsuitable for long
vehicles'. ⑧ Turn R at T-junction. ⑨ At FP sign turn L through
gap and walk alongside hedge on R. At far corner of second
field turn L (FP sign) alongside hedge. In 100 yds turn R through
gap to walk along LH side of old wall. Follow this wall through
four fields to waymarked stile at corner. ⑩ Turn R to fence-
stile, descend steeply
and turn L to follow
valley down to wood.
Keep straight on through
wood on clear path to
stile onto road. ⑪ Turn
R up road. (At
this point you'll
wish you'd ignored
the author's
advice not to
park in the
village).

Lowdales

38

St. Peter's Church, Hackness

HACKNESS

HACKNESS has close associations with St. Hilda, Abbess of Whitby, who in 680 AD decreed that a small monastery be built here to serve as a place of relaxation for the monks and nuns of Whitby. Invading Danes destroyed the monastery in 867, but it was rebuilt in 1095 and functioned until the Dissolution in 1539. The only surviving remains are its lake and pieces of a Saxon cross (now in the church). St. Peter's Church is a lovely building, despite having been extensively reconstructed in conflicting architectural styles. The oldest parts date from 1050. The church contains a memorial to Lady Margaret Hoby, the first woman diarist, who died in 1633. She was Lady of the Manor of Hackness, and her famous diary now reposes in the British Museum. Set in spacious grounds close to the church is Hackness Hall, an elegant Georgian mansion designed by the eminent architect John Carr of York.

The deciduous HILDA WOOD in all probability takes its name from St. Hilda. The wood harbours a rich variety of wild flowers, and turns white in early summer when masses of ramsons (wild garlic) produce their starry, pungent-smelling blossoms.

A welcome sight at Reasty Bank

O.S. MAPS : Landranger Series (1 : 50 000) Sheet 94 (Whitby)
Outdoor Leisure 27 (1 : 25 000) SE Sheet

© Jack Keighley 1993

(14)

ST. GREGORY'S MINSTER

6½ MILES

Close to the busy A170, and yet in a setting of serene tranquillity, stands a little gem of a church. St. Gregory's Minster dates back to pre-Conquest days and is a place of absorbing interest. Nearby is Kirkdale Cave, famed for its yields of the bones and teeth of prehistoric fauna. This is a predominantly woodland walk of quite exceptional beauty.

St. Gregory's Minster

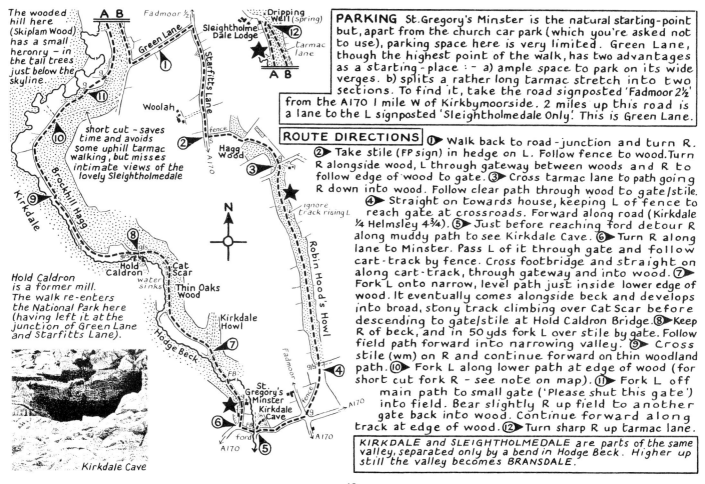

The wooded hill here (Skiplam Wood) has a small heronry – in the tall trees just below the skyline.

A B
Fadmoor ½
Green Lane
①
Dripping Well (spring)
Sleightholme Dale Lodge
⑫
tarmac lane
A B

Woolah
⑪
Starfitts Lane
fence
②
Hagg Wood
③
short cut – saves time and avoids some uphill tarmac walking, but misses intimate views of the lovely Sleightholmedale
⑩
Brockhill Hagg
Kirkdale
A170
ignore track rising L
⑨
⑧
gls
Hold Caldron
Cat Scar
water sinks
Thin Oaks Wood
Robin Hood's Howl
N

Hold Caldron is a former mill. The walk re-enters the National Park here (having left it at the junction of Green Lane and Starfitts Lane).

Kirkdale Howl
Hodge Beck
⑦
Fadmoor
gls
④
fence
gls
A170
FB
St. Gregory's Minster
Kirkdale Cave
⑥
FB
ford
A170
⑤
A170

Kirkdale Cave

PARKING St. Gregory's Minster is the natural starting-point but, apart from the church car park (which you're asked not to use), parking space here is very limited. Green Lane, though the highest point of the walk, has two advantages as a starting-place :– a) ample space to park on its wide verges. b) splits a rather long tarmac stretch into two sections. To find it, take the road signposted 'Fadmoor 2½' from the A170 1 mile W of Kirkbymoorside. 2 miles up this road is a lane to the L signposted 'Sleightholmedale Only'. This is Green Lane.

ROUTE DIRECTIONS ① Walk back to road-junction and turn R. ② Take stile (FP sign) in hedge on L. Follow fence to wood. Turn R alongside wood, L through gateway between woods and R to follow edge of wood to gate. ③ Cross tarmac lane to path going R down into wood. Follow clear path through wood to gate/stile. ④ Straight on towards house, keeping L of fence to reach gate at crossroads. Forward along road (Kirkdale ¼ Helmsley 4¾). ⑤ Just before reaching ford detour R along muddy path to see Kirkdale Cave. ⑥ Turn R along lane to Minster. Pass L of it through gate and follow cart-track by fence. Cross footbridge and straight on along cart-track, through gateway and into wood. ⑦ Fork L onto narrow, level path just inside lower edge of wood. It eventually comes alongside beck and develops into broad, stony track climbing over Cat Scar before descending to gate/stile at Hold Caldron Bridge. ⑧ Keep R of beck, and in 50 yds fork L over stile by gate. Follow field path forward into narrowing valley. ⑨ Cross stile (wm) on R and continue forward on thin woodland path. ⑩ Fork L along lower path at edge of wood (for short cut fork R – see note on map). ⑪ Fork L off main path to small gate ('Please shut this gate') into field. Bear slightly R up field to another gate back into wood. Continue forward along track at edge of wood. ⑫ Turn sharp R up tarmac lane.

KIRKDALE and SLEIGHTHOLMEDALE are parts of the same valley, separated only by a bend in Hodge Beck. Higher up still the valley becomes BRANSDALE.

ST. GREGORY'S MINSTER

was rebuilt c 1055, the original church (founded 654 AD) having been destroyed by marauding Danes. There is much to interest the visitor, including an unusually narrow Saxon doorway, some fine Saxon coffin stones and stone benches around the interior walls provided for the old and infirm before pews were introduced. (It is said that this gave rise to the expression 'Let the weakest go to the wall'). The piece de résistance, however, is the Saxon sundial in the porch, above the south door. This 7' slab of stone, discovered beneath a layer of plaster during 1771 building work, has the longest surviving inscription in stone from Saxon times.

'ORM GAMAL'S SON BOUGHT ST. GREGORY'S MINSTER WHEN IT WAS ALL BROKEN DOWN AND FALLEN AND HE LET IT BE MADE ANEW FROM THE GROUND TO CHRIST AND ST. GREGORY, IN EDWARD'S DAYS, THE KING AND IN TOSTI'S DAYS, THE EARL. THIS IS DAY'S SUN MARKER AT EVERY TIDE. AND HAWORTH, ME WROUGHT AND BRAND PRIEST.

'Edward' is Edward the Confessor, King of England 1042 - 66, and 'Tosti' refers to Tostig, Earl of Northumberland.

KIRKDALE CAVES

A series of interconnecting muddy passages. To reach the entrance, some 10' up a cliff face, entails an awkward, slippery scramble. A section of cave discovered by quarrymen in 1821 was found to contain remains of numerous animals, including bison, bear, giant deer, hippopotamus, mammoth, lion, rhinoceros and wolf. It was deduced that, in prehistoric times (up to 100,000 years ago), the cave had been a hyena den.

O.S. MAPS: Landranger Series (1 : 50 000) Sheet 100 (Malton and Pickering)   Outdoor Leisure 26 (1 : 25 000) SW Sheet

© Jack Keighley 1993

THE LITTLEBECK VALLEY

6 MILES

A walk of extreme beauty throughout, but the first 2¾ miles, from the picturesque hamlet of Littlebeck and by way of Falling Foss, one of Yorkshire's loveliest waterfalls, to the ruins of John Bond's Sheep House, is veritably a journey through Paradise. Some open moorland on the return route provides a sharp, but pleasing, contrast. Easy going - no steep gradients.

Old Wife's Neck   John Cross

Be thankful that you finish the walk DOWN the tarmac lane, which was probably given its name by those unfortunates who had to walk UP it!

PARKING At Littlebeck, 2 miles SE of Sleights. Car park by the Village Hall at E end of hamlet.
Map ref: 880 050

ROUTE DIRECTIONS

①▶ From car park walk L down road. At first bend turn L through small gate (signed FALLING FOSS) and follow excellent path (stepped in places) through wood. ②▶ At The Hermitage take LH (upper) path and in 100yds fork R (SP c TO c). ③▶ Fork R again (SP C TO c) to descend to Midge Hall. Cross footbridge on L to road. ④▶ Turn L over road bridge then R to follow beckside path. ⑤▶ Fork R to cross footbridge over tributary stream. ⑥▶ At May Beck car park keep straight on along LH side of stream (choice of two paths which soon unite). Follow clear path up valley, crossing stream several times. ⑦▶ At large sheepfold ford stream, turn L up to guidepost and L again towards forest. ⑧▶ Cross stile in wire fence and follow broad path L up moor. Path runs roughly parallel with forest on L. ⑨▶ At guidepost turn L to swing-gate in wall. Descend cart-track, which swings R to follow fence to road. ⑩▶ Turn L down road. ⑪▶ When road bends L turn R (FP sign). Keep R of wood, and at guidepost turn L between wood and fence. Keep to top side of wood to reach stile in crosswall. ⑫▶ Continue forward, with old fence on R. Soon the path crosses a stile to continue along RH side of fence. ⑬▶ Follow cart-track (wm) between fences to gate, and keep straight on across field to another gate. ⑭▶ Turn R up tarmac lane. ⑮▶ Immediately after passing house turn L (FP sign) onto broad green path. Cross farm road to keep straight ahead along clear path with wall on L. ⑯▶ Turn L down steep tarmac lane.

Midge Hall—once a keeper's cottage

Map labels: Moorside Farm, Lousy Hill Lane, LITTLEBECK, Meth Ch, Cave, ford, spoil heaps (alum mines), Little Beck, farm road, farm, heather, peat, The Hermitage, Lodge, Forest Trail, Falling Foss Midge Hall, car park, May Beck, May Beck Farm, pond, wall, fence, peat, road, ruin, John Cross, Shooting House Rigg, car park (ice-cream sometimes), Alans Seat, Hunters Steean (stone FB), Old Wife's Neck, earthwork, A169, B1416 (A171)

N

NOTE:
Two sections of this walk (④–⑦ and ⑨–⑩) are on concessionary paths rather than official rights-of-way.

Inset map labels (A–B): slab bridge, heather, slab bridge, John Bond's Sheep House, FB, Blea Hill Beck

JOHN BOND'S SHEEP HOUSE, now in ruins, was a large and complex sheepfold. The stone-walled enclosures were used for sorting sheep at shearing time and for collecting the flock prior to bringing the sheep down from the moor to the farm.

JOHN CROSS was a wayside cross of early Christian origin. Only the base-stone is original, the shaft having probably been destroyed by 17thC. Puritans. The stone now inserted into the base is an old Sneaton-Fylingdales boundary marker.

42

LITTLEBECK is a tiny hamlet deep set in a most beautifully wooded valley and centred upon a ford, from which the lane climbs very steeply on either side. A chalet-style building just above the Methodist Church is the workshop of a local woodcarver whose trademark is a gnome.

•—•—•—•

FALLING FOSS will be heard before it is seen, for this beautiful waterfall, which can be spectacular after heavy rainfall, is partially hidden by foliage. Local literature contains remarkable discrepancies in estimating its height as anything between 30 and 60 feet. The lowest figure is probably about right.

THE HERMITAGE is a most interesting curio. A mason named Jeffrey is thought to have hollowed out this enormous boulder. 'GC 1790' above the doorway refers to George Chubb, a local schoolmaster. Be sure to sample the comfort of the rooftop rock seats.

THE SMALL POND to the L of the path just beyond point ⑤ supports a diverse population of aquatic creatures, including smooth newts, tadpoles, pond snails, water boatmen, dragonfly larvae and whirligig beetles.

The moorland track on Shooting House Rigg between points ⑧ and ⑨ cuts through four linear banks and ditches. Their age and purpose can only be guessed at, but it is thought that they are of Bronze Age origin – perhaps relics of a settlement's defensive system. 30 yards to the L is OLD WIFE'S NECK, a standing-stone which resembles the head and shoulders of a woman.

O.S. MAPS : Landranger Series (1 : 50 000) Sheet 94 (Whitby)
Outdoor Leisure 27 (1 : 25 000) NE Sheet

© Jack Keighley 1993

⑯

OSMOTHERLEY & BEACON HILL

5½ MILES

This fine walk, at the western extremity of the Cleveland Hills, offers a rich variety of terrain and scenery, incorporating forest and woodland tracks, farm pastures and heather- and bracken-clad moors. From the attractive and pleasantly somnolent village of Osmotherley the steady climb of 450' to Beacon Hill provides extensive views across the plains to the west and north.

the path into Osmotherley

JKeighley

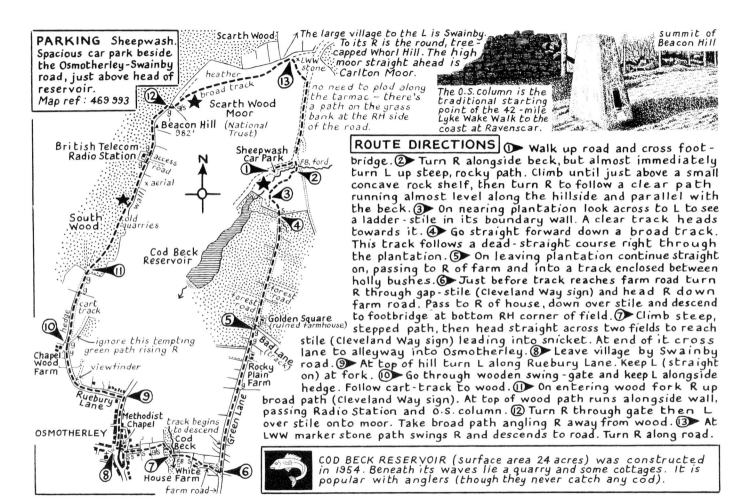

PARKING Sheepwash. Spacious car park beside the Osmotherley-Swainby road, just above head of reservoir. Map ref: 469 993

Scarth Wood

The large village to the L is Swainby. To its R is the round, tree-capped Whorl Hill. The high moor straight ahead is Carlton Moor.

no need to plod along the tarmac – there's a path on the grass bank at the RH side of the road.

summit of Beacon Hill

The O.S. column is the traditional starting point of the 42-mile Lyke Wake Walk to the coast at Ravenscar.

heather
broad track
LWW stone

Scarth Wood Moor (National Trust)

Beacon Hill 982'

British Telecom Radio Station

access road

x aerial

South Wood
old quarries

N

Sheepwash Car Park
FB, ford

Cod Beck Reservoir

forest road
forest road

Golden Square (ruined farmhouse)

Bad Lane (track)

Green Lane

Rocky Plain Farm

cart track
hedge

ignore this tempting green path rising R

Chapel Wood Farm

viewfinder

Ruebury Lane

Methodist Chapel

track begins to descend Cod Beck

OSMOTHERLEY

White House Farm

farm road

ROUTE DIRECTIONS

① Walk up road and cross foot-bridge. ② Turn R alongside beck, but almost immediately turn L up steep, rocky path. Climb until just above a small concave rock shelf, then turn R to follow a clear path running almost level along the hillside and parallel with the beck. ③ On nearing plantation look across to L to see a ladder-stile in its boundary wall. A clear track heads towards it. ④ Go straight forward down a broad track. This track follows a dead-straight course right through the plantation. ⑤ On leaving plantation continue straight on, passing to R of farm and into a track enclosed between holly bushes. ⑥ Just before track reaches farm road turn R through gap-stile (Cleveland Way sign) and head R down farm road. Pass to R of house, down over stile and descend to footbridge at bottom RH corner of field. ⑦ Climb steep, stepped path, then head straight across two fields to reach stile (Cleveland Way sign) leading into snicket. At end of it cross lane to alleyway into Osmotherley. ⑧ Leave village by Swainby road. ⑨ At top of hill turn L along Ruebury Lane. Keep L (straight on) at fork. ⑩ Go through wooden swing-gate and keep L alongside hedge. Follow cart-track to wood. ⑪ On entering wood fork R up broad path (Cleveland Way sign). At top of wood path runs alongside wall, passing Radio Station and O.S. column. ⑫ Turn R through gate then L over stile onto moor. Take broad path angling R away from wood. ⑬ At LWW marker stone path swings R and descends to road. Turn R along road.

COD BECK RESERVOIR (surface area 24 acres) was constructed in 1954. Beneath its waves lie a quarry and some cottages. It is popular with anglers (though they never catch any cod).

44

NOTE: The walk is inclined to be muddy, particularly on the woodland paths. The track through the plantation (points ④ to ⑤) may be badly churned up by forestry vehicles.

OSMOTHERLEY

Market cross and Golden Lion Inn

The centrepiece of this pretty village is the small green with its market cross and stone table. The cross was erected in 1874 to replace a much older one. Weekly markets were held here until 1823, and the table would be used as a butter stall, fish stall or barter table. John Wesley preached here, and the Methodist chapel is one of England's oldest (1754).

ST. PETER'S CHURCH displays an assortment of Anglo-Danish stones in its porch and has many other interesting features – notably a fine Norman doorway, 13thC font, 14thC chancel arch and some lovely stained glass. THE QUEEN CATHERINE INN is named after Catherine Parr, Henry VIII's sixth and final spouse (*), who hailed from this neck of the woods. * If you get bored with the walk, try thinking of the names (in order) and fates of the other five. Answers below - no peeping.

stone at point ⑬

An information board on the monstrous RADIO STATION states that BT *'have kept the size of the aerials to a minimum so as not to detract from the beauty of the National Park.'* Thank heaven for that! The mind boggles as to what the result would have been had they not felt disposed to exercise such commendable restraint.

Answers : 1. Catherine of Aragon (divorced). 2. Anne Boleyn (executed). 3. Jane Seymour (died). 4. Anne of Cleves (divorced). 5. Catherine Howard (executed).

O.S. MAPS : (Edge of map problems) Landranger Series (1:50 000) Sheets 93 (Middlesbrough and Darlington), 99 (Northallerton and Ripon) and 100 (Malton and Pickering) Outdoor Leisure 26 (1:25 000) NW and SW Sheets

⑰

CAPTAIN COOK'S COASTLINE

6½ MILES

In 1745 James Cook arrived in Staithes as a lad to be apprenticed to a local draper, and it was this quaint hotch-potch of a fishing-port, with its rugged coastal scenery, which inspired his love of the sea. From Runswick Bay a gentle inland walk through attractively wooded countryside precedes an exhilarating cliff-top return from Staithes.

Staithes

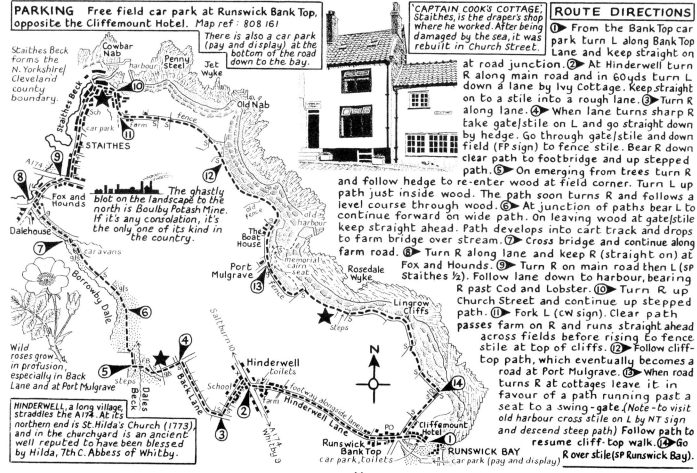

PARKING Free field car park at Runswick Bank Top, opposite the Cliffemount Hotel. Map ref : 808 161

There is also a car park (pay and display) at the bottom of the road down to the bay.

Staithes Beck forms the N. Yorkshire/ Cleveland county boundary.

Cowbar Nab

harbour Penny Steel

Jet Wyke

Sch

car park

STAITHES

A174

Fox and Hounds

Dalehouse

caravans

Wild roses grow in profusion, especially in Back Lane and at Port Mulgrave.

Borrowby Dale

Old Nab

The ghastly blot on the landscape to the north is Boulby Potash Mine. If it's any consolation, it's the only one of its kind in the country.

old fence

old harbour

The Boat House

Port Mulgrave

memorial cairn seat

fence

Rosedale Wyke

Lingrow Cliffs

steps

N

Saltburn 10

Back Lane

Dales Beck

steps

School

FB

Hinderwell
toilets

footway alongside lane

farm

Hinderwell Lane

A174 Whitby 9

HINDERWELL, a long village, straddles the A174. At its northern end is St. Hilda's Church (1773), and in the churchyard is an ancient well reputed to have been blessed by Hilda, 7th C. Abbess of Whitby.

PO

Runswick Bank Top car park, toilets

Cliffemount Hotel

RUNSWICK BAY

car park (pay and display)

'CAPTAIN COOK'S COTTAGE', Staithes, is the draper's shop where he worked. After being damaged by the sea, it was rebuilt in Church Street.

ROUTE DIRECTIONS

① From the Bank Top car park turn L along Bank Top Lane and keep straight on at road junction. **②** At Hinderwell turn R along main road and in 60yds turn L down a lane by Ivy Cottage. Keep straight on to a stile into a rough lane. **③** Turn R along lane. **④** When lane turns sharp R take gate/stile on L and go straight down by hedge. Go through gate/stile and down field (FP sign) to fence stile. Bear R down clear path to footbridge and up stepped path. **⑤** On emerging from trees turn R and follow hedge to re-enter wood at field corner. Turn L up path just inside wood. The path soon turns R and follows a level course through wood. **⑥** At junction of paths bear L to continue forward on wide path. On leaving wood at gate/stile keep straight ahead. Path develops into cart track and drops to farm bridge over stream. **⑦** Cross bridge and continue along farm road. **⑧** Turn R along lane and keep R (straight on) at Fox and Hounds. **⑨** Turn R on main road then L (SP Staithes ½). Follow lane down to harbour, bearing R past Cod and Lobster. **⑩** Turn R up Church Street and continue up stepped path. **⑪** Fork L (cw sign). Clear path passes farm on R and runs straight ahead across fields before rising to fence stile at top of cliffs. **⑫** Follow cliff-top path, which eventually becomes a road at Port Mulgrave. **⑬** When road turns R at cottages leave it in favour of a path running past a seat to a swing-gate. (Note - to visit old harbour cross stile on L by NT sign and descend steep path) Follow path to resume cliff-top walk. **⑭** Go R over stile (SP Runswick Bay).

RUNSWICK BAY The lower part of the village is quite delightful, with its bright, pantiled cottages clustered chaotically on the steep hillside above the bay. Charming pathways wind between the pretty gardens of what were once fishermen's homes; now many are holiday cottages, for the local fishing industry died in 1950 after some 30 years of decline. One tragic night in 1664 a huge landslip caused the entire original village (save for one house) to disappear into the sea.

STAITHES, though heavily into tourism, still retains an olde-worlde charm. The old lobster port still has its *cobles* – Viking-style boats with high, sharp prows and broad beams – albeit they are now powered by inboard engines rather than sails and oars. Staithes has weathered many violent storms. The Cod and Lobster has been damaged by the sea on numerous occasions, the last being on 31 Jan, 1953, when the kitchen,

scullery and two bedrooms were destroyed. The walls are now reinforced with steel rods. Smuggling was rife along this coast in the 18th and early 19th centuries.

PORT MULGRAVE A steep path known as 'Wilf's Way' (a memorial cairn near the top gives details) leads down to the tiny harbour, which was constructed in the 1850s to receive iron-ore for shipment up the coast to the large ironworks. The ore arrived through a mile-long tunnel (the blocked entrance can still be seen) Disused since 1916, the harbour is now crumbling.

memorial cairn

Cook, James (1728-79) English navigator. Son of farm labourer. Joined Royal Navy and gained high reputation for scientific skill. Commanded *Endeavour, Resolution* and *Adventure* on great voyages of discovery to Australia and New Zealand. Also surveyed the coast of Newfoundland. Murdered at Hawaii whilst attempting to find north-west passage.

O.S. MAPS : Landranger Series (1 : 50 000) Sheet 94 (Whitby) Outdoor Leisure 27 (1 : 25 000) NE Sheet

© Jack Keighley 1993

CROSSCLIFF & THE BRIDESTONES

4½ MILES

The Forest Drive (a 9-mile-long toll road) affords an opportunity to sample the scenic beauty of the Dalby Forest without putting a foot to the ground. Very few visitors, however, will dash through without pausing to acquaint themselves more intimately with some of the forest's many attractions. Of the wealth of walks available, the one here described is the loveliest and most varied

Bridestones Moor

PARKING Take the Dalby Forest Drive which leaves the Thornton-le-Dale to Whitby road 1½ miles N of Thornton. Motor for 4½ miles along this scenic route and park at Staindale Lake car park.
Map ref: 878 905
Alternatively use the High Staindale car park ½ mile further on at the head of the lake. <u>Note</u>: The forest drive is a toll road – fee £2 per vehicle.

| ROUTE DIRECTIONS | ① From Staindale Lake car park take the path which descends to the beck and continues upstream on its LH side (don't cross the footbridge). On approaching the lake dam the path veers L to rejoin the Forest Drive. ② Turn R and follow the tarmac lakeside path. At far end of lake keep straight on across car park. ③ Turn L along Forest Drive and at hairpin bend turn R between buildings to follow 'Walk to Crosscliff' (blue arrows).

The attractive STAINDALE LAKE provides a picturesque setting for a picnic. It is an artificial lake created in 1976 to attract a greater variety of wildlife to the area.

Keep L (straight on) at fork along broad cart track. ④ Fork L (blue arrow) onto grassy track which narrows as it climbs a shallow gully. ⑤ At forest road turn L and in 10yds turn R up path following line of ancient dikes. Keep straight on along broad track to reach view indicator at Crosscliff. ⑥ Turn L to follow broad, level path along top of escarpment. ⑦ Where 'blue trail' is waymarked along track branching L continue ahead (yellow arrow) along the escarpment. ⑧ As end of forest comes into view, look out for an old right-of-way crossing track (marked by 4-way yellow arrow sign and pair of old gateposts on R). Turn L and follow it through trees to fence-stile onto open moor. Turn L along a broad track through heather. ⑨ At a slight depression are six silver birches to the R of the track. Pass these, then turn R onto a narrow, but clear, path in the heather, heading towards the trees of Bridestones Griff. ⑩ At a small cairn turn R down a path which descends to a broad, cobbled path. Turn R along it to visit High Bridestones. ⑪ Return along cobbled path, which leads directly (don't go back up to cairn) to Low Bridestones. ⑫ At last Bridestone ignore broad path heading L. Continue along path towards wood. Broad path leads down through wood to stile. Descend L to car park.

Map labels: old gateposts · Grime Moor · fence · broad track in heather · Crosscliff Brow · young plantation · High Bridestones · ⑧ · ⑪ · ⑨ · ⑩ · ⑦ · ⑥ · Crosscliff Wood · Dovedale Griff · Bridestones Griff · blue trail · broad level path · viewpoint · Dargate Dikes · Yondhead Rigg · Low Bridestones · ⑫ · fence · Low wood · Staindale Beck · Jonathan Gill · toilets · High Staindale Car Park · ⑤ · forest road · Dargate Slack · ④ · pond · Grain Slack · Grain Beck · ② · ③ · Staindale Lake · ① · Staindale Lake Car Park · Forest Drive · Low Dalby

High Staindale Car Park has a rather charming Bird Feeding Station

N

OPENING TIMES
Dalby Forest is open all the year round. Low Dalby Visitor Centre is open Easter to September/October 11·00 am to 5·00 pm. Annual Passes are available for using the Forest Drive at a cost of £10. School parties and coaches are welcome by appointment. Teachers' information packs available. Contact: Forest District Office, 42 Eastgate, Pickering YO18 7DU (0751) 72771 or Low Dalby Visitor Centre (0751) 60295

48

DALBY FOREST 🌲🌲🌲🌲🌲

Among the 6,000,000 trees growing on the forest's 1,500 acres are some 15 species of conifers and 22 species of broadleaved trees and shrubs. The 150,000 people who visit Dalby each year may enjoy, in addition to the forest's natural beauty, a wealth of facilities including scenic picnic sites and over 60 miles of waymarked trails. Low Dalby, a Forestry Commission village built in 1949, has an excellent and informative Visitor Centre which should not be missed. Dalby has some 30 miles of maintained forest roads, and each year stages 5 motor car and 2 motor cycle rallies. The forest provides a valuable wildlife habitat. A wide variety of mammals, deer and badgers included, make their home here, as do over 80 species of birds. Crossbills and siskins nest in the forest, and the tiny goldcrest, Britain's smallest bird, is quite common, but perhaps the most interesting feathered resident is the strange, nocturnal nightjar, whose 'churring' call sounds like a distant motorbike.

THE BRIDESTONES
, a famous feature of the National Park, are outcrops of Jurassic sandstone made up of alternating layers of hard and softer rock. Weather erosion over the past 60,000 years has sculpted these huge blocks into fantastic shapes. Though it has been suggested that the stones may have been the scene of ancient marriage rites, it is more likely that their name is derived from the Norse 'Brinkstones' or edge stones. The moor, owned by the National Trust since 1944, was established as a Nature Reserve in 1966.

TWO ODD BEAKS
Crossbill *Nightjar*

The beaks of birds tell us a great deal about the way they feed. Some have become highly specialised, and these are two of the most bizarre. The crossbill looks as though it has flown into a wall, but its twisted mandibles are perfect for splitting open cones to extract the seeds. The nightjar has hardly any beak at all, but can open its mouth very wide – literally from ear to ear – with a wide fringe of bristles spreading out on each side. Thus equipped, it feeds at twilight by flying around with its mouth agape to catch moths.

O.S. MAPS : *Landranger Series (1:50 000) Sheet 94 (Whitby)*
Outdoor Leisure 27 (1:25 000) S.E. Sheet

© Jack Keighley 1993

---

⑲

ACROSS HOGRAH MOOR
(TWICE!)
6½ MILES

Some of the National Park's most glorious heather moorland is that which enfolds the secluded village of Westerdale, from where this walk begins. The scenery, though predominantly moorland, is surprisingly varied, and there are lovely views down into the sequestered and little-known valley of Baysdale. Undulating terrain, with no steep climbing.

stone footbridge, Great Hograh Beck

JKeighley

49

the memorial cairn above Great Hograh Beck

ROUTE DIRECTIONS

①▶ Leave Westerdale by the lane with the telephone kiosk near the church. ②▶ 100 yds past Youth Hostel take stile (FP sign) in hedge atop low wall on R. Bear L (no path) across field (aim towards house with red pantile roof on far hillside) to reach gate (FP sign). Descend cart-track, which turns R down to footbridge. Cross bridge. ③▶ Follow LH field boundary to metal gate at hedge corner. Up centre of next field (no path) to gate/stile (wm) then head for house. ④▶ Cross stile into garden and go through gate (wm) at LH end of buildings. Turn R alongside fence then L to climb by wall. Cross wall at stile in recess and continue to follow it uphill. ⑤▶ Turn R along tarmac road. In 150 yds turn L (BW sign) onto narrow path in bracken. Follow cairned track across moor. ⑥▶ Cross stone footbridge and immediately turn R on path downstream. Path bears L away from stream and soon joins a broad track which eventually descends by edge of plantation to The Low House. ⑦▶ Straight through garden to stile (wm). Keep straight on, with wall on R. ⑧▶ Cross step-stile at wall corner and continue forward, with wall now on L, to Thorntree House. ⑨▶ Turn L up cart-track to gate and follow broad track up through plantation, to gate at top. ⑩▶ Turn L on path alongside forest. ⑪▶ Pass through gateway in crosswall and turn R to follow clear path curving L over hill. ⑫▶ Just past grouse butt fork R onto lesser path down to stone footbridge. Return across moor. ⑬▶ On reaching tarmac road cross it and continue forward on sketchy path to another tarmac road. Turn R along it. ⑭▶ Cross stile on L (FP sign) by farm entrance. Follow hedge down to WESTERDALE packhorse bridge. Rejoin road.

A GLANCE AT THE MAP WILL REVEAL THAT THIS IS NOT A TRUE CIRCULAR WALK, BUT TWO SMALL CIRCULAR BITS CONNECTED BY A LINEAR MOORLAND PATH WHICH HAS TO BE WALKED TWICE. THIS IN NO WAY DETRACTS FROM THE WALK'S MERIT – INDEED IT PROVIDES THE BONUS OF TWO VISITS TO THE LITTLE BRIDGE OVER GREAT HOGRAH BECK. THIS ENCHANTING SPOT – ONE OF THE AUTHOR'S FAVOURITE PLACES IN THE NORTH YORK MOORS – IS AS NEAR TO A FAIRY GLADE AS ANYTHING YOU'RE EVER LIKELY TO SEE.

50

WESTERDALE

Christ Church   Westerdale

The first village on the Esk, which rises at Esklets 2½ miles to the south-west. The ornate Hall has been a Youth Hostel since 1947, but was built as a hunting lodge in the 1840s. The attractive church was rebuilt in 1838. Hunters' Sty Bridge is a medieval packhorse bridge which was restored (somewhat un-sympathetically) in 1874. Note the Duncombe family coronet on its parapet.

This extraordinary monument stands in the garden of a cottage at the south end of Westerdale village. It was placed there in 1727 by one Thomas Bulmer, a mariner, and the lettering which covers the entire shaft tells of the many countries he visited and, in copious detail, of how he survived a shipwreck.

BAYSDALE

IS A QUIET, SECLUDED VALLEY WITH NO THROUGH MOTOR ROAD. A FARM IN THE VALLEY OCCUPIES THE SITE OF A CISTERCIAN NUNNERY (founded c 1189) WHICH HAS DISAPPEARED ALMOST WITHOUT TRACE ; A SMALL MEDIEVAL BRIDGE AND A FEW SCULPTURED STONES ARE ALL THAT REMAIN.

O.S. MAPS :   Landranger Series (1 : 50 000) Sheet 94 (Whitby)
                 Outdoor Leisure 26 (1 : 25 000) NW Sheet

© Jack Keighley 1993

20

SINNINGTON & APPLETON-LE-MOORS

4¾ MILES

A short, leisurely stroll around a lovely stretch of the sparkling River Seven at the extreme southern edge of the National Park. The walk links two villages which, though equally attractive and peaceful, differ considerably in layout and have greatly contrasting churches. Delightful shady paths wind through glorious woodland which is especially beautiful when carpeted with spring flowers.

The Green, Sinnington

ROUTE DIRECTIONS ① From the village green set off along the road signed 'No Through Road' passing to R of maypole. ② Keep straight on at another 'No Through Road' sign (but detour up lane to R to visit church and hall). When tarmac ends at Over Beck Cottage keep L (straight on). ③ Ignore BW going L with river. Follow broad track at edge of wood. ④ At crosstracks go straight on, passing through gate/stile to a green meadow path. ⑤ At a prominent tree the path swings up R, then L to stile into wood. Continue forward on good path. ⑥ Path runs along RH side of hedge at bottom edge of wood. At fork go R up steep path (not officially a right-of-way, but a commonly-used short cut). ⑦ On reaching a broad crosstrack turn R along it, but in 10 yds turn L onto a path which develops into a broad track descending to a gate. Follow path between hedges to another gate. ⑧ Turn L (SP Appleton le Moors). Cross footbridge and turn L to follow field boundary round to gate onto farm road. ⑨ Go straight on up farm road. ⑩ At end of farm road continue straight ahead along tarmac lane. Turn L at T-junction to walk through village. ⑪ At bottom of village street go straight on down farm track (BW sign). Pass through gate and follow path down RH side of fields. ⑫ Go through gate (wm) set at an angle in the hedge. Turn ½ R across field to gate into wood. ⑬ Turn L to follow clear path through wood to gate. ⑭ On leaving wood turn L along broad track which follows river back to Sinnington.

FOOTPATH DIVERSIONS IN THE VICINITY OF APPLETON MILL FARM MEAN THAT THE RIVER IS NOW SPANNED BY A BIG NEW FOOTBRIDGE. THOUGH SPLENDIDLY CONSTRUCTED, THIS BRIDGE LACKS THE RUSTIC CHARM OF THE OLD MILL WEIR, WHICH WAS THE PREVIOUS CROSSING PLACE.

THE RIVER SEVEN is born at Rosedale Head, and has flowed for some 12 miles by the time it leaves the National Park at Sinnington. The beautiful riverside woodlands hereabouts provide home and shelter for a rich variety of mammals, birds and insects, and produce lovely displays of wild flowers in spring and summer. Early bloomers include primrose, violet and wood anemone, which normally flower in March, and these are followed in April by wood sorrel, ramsons (wild garlic) and sweet woodruff. Later still, in May and June, will come the glory of the bluebells.

After leaving Sinnington the Seven meanders peacefully southwards for another 6 miles to join the Rye at Little Habton.

wood anemone

HONEY FOR SALE

sign in the garden of Over Beck Cottage, the last house passed on the way out of Sinnington.

SINNINGTON

Mercifully by-passed by the A170, this pretty riverside village lies peaceful and serene, its slumber undisturbed by the roar of high-speed traffic. With a history dating back to Viking times, Sinnington retains its olde-worlde charm and has some fine old buildings clustered around a spacious green where plump ducks brazenly pester visitors for titbits. The river bridge was built in 1767, but of greater interest is the oddly-sited little packhorse bridge in the centre of the green. The

All Saints, Sinnington

fox on the nearby Maypole reminds us that the Sinnington Hunt (founded 1745 and one of England's oldest) meets here. The church, though much-restored in 1904, still contains some Saxon and Norman features. If the village lives up to its name the vicar will be kept fully occupied! Just above the church is a barn which was originally a 12th.C. hall. Unfortunately the appearance of this hoary old building has scarcely been enhanced by the erection of an ugly, adjoining wooden barn. ✿✿

APPLETON-LE-MOORS is a village with a typically medieval layout – a broad main street with a row of houses and a back lane on either side. The village, and indeed the surrounding countryside, is dominated by the 90' spire of Christ Church. This unusual church was built in 1866 in a richly decorative French Gothic style.

These three dubious characters will be watching you walk through the village

LOW CROSS, an ancient waymarker stone

O.S. MAPS : Landranger Series (1:50 000) Sheet 100 (Malton, Pickering)
Outdoor Leisure (1:25 000) 26 SW Sheet and 27 SE Sheet
© Jack Keighley 1993

㉑

THE HEART OF ROSEDALE

6½ MILES

Picturesque Rosedale – it is hard to credit that a valley now so serene and pastoral could once have been a booming iron-mining centre. The industry died in the 1920s, but the forsaken relics remain to add interest to the beauty of a walk embracing colourful moors and flowery riverside meadows. Fairly strenuous, so allow plenty of time.

ruins of Gill Bank

PARKING Rosedale Abbey. Two car parks in village, near Milburn Arms Hotel.   Map ref: 725 960

The holiday cottages are named after ponies

ROUTE DIRECTIONS ①▶ Cross village, with green on L, towards church and school. Continue forward to L of school and bear R along road. ②▶ On L you will see a house with FP sign on either side of it. Take second of these (step-stile) and turn R along caravan-site drive. Keep to main drive (FP signs). ③▶ At covered well bear R off drive (FP sign), through swing-gate and forward alongside hedge on L. As path nears river, cross stile to enter wood and turn L over footbridge. Go through small gate and up field to ladder-stile. ④▶ Turn R to follow tarmac road. ⑤▶ 30yds after crossing bridge turn L (steps and FP sign) through stile. Climb alongside hedge to steps and gateway, and straight on up narrow field to gap in broken wall. ⑥▶ Turn L up green path, and in a few yards fork R. After passing ruined farm bear slightly R up steep grassy spur between walls. Make for stile at top RH corner of enclosure. ⑦▶ Turn R to follow wall, but when it turns away keep straight on (sketchy path). Skirt round depression, and after crossing two small gullies turn L to climb grassy strip of moor. ⑧▶ Turn R on trackbed of old railway. ⑨▶ Note position of some ruins up on L. They will disappear from view, but estimate when you're abreast of them and turn sharp R down clear path. Note roofs of farm buildings below, and aim well to R of them to locate ladder-stile. ⑩▶ Turn L to pass guidepost and straight on through gate. Cross farm road and straight down field to cross foot-bridge. ⑪▶ Turn L and climb to gate in crossfence. Keep straight on to pass through farmyard. ⑫▶ Turn R along tarmac road. ⑬▶ Turn L at far end of row of cottages, then R over fence-stile (FP sign). Head towards buildings in trees on skyline. Cross small stream and climb, with wall on L, to gateway. ⑭▶ Follow power-line up field then swing R towards farm, but before reaching it cross stile (wm) in wire fence on L and follow path slanting R up bank to stile onto road. ⑮▶ Turn R along road, and in 40 yds take gate on L (BW sign). Turn L on track descending to gate. Don't use gate – turn R down green track passing to R of small reservoir. ⑯▶ At end of reservoir fence fork to L of old wall and descend to ladder-stile. Maintain direction to gate onto farm road. ⑰▶ Turn L and immediately R (FP sign) to walk downstream to footbridge. ⑱▶ Follow direction of BW sign up bank to locate small gate in

The middle section of the walk gives good views of the rows of kilns of Rosedale East Mines. Note the line of the branch railway which served them. The terraced Hill Cottages were formerly miners' dwellings.

This short cut is not an official right-of-way, but saves an awful lot of time and energy

ruins · The Alders · High House Farm · R. Seven · Craven Garth Farm · Bottoms Farm · reservoir · ⑫ · ⑭ · ⑮ · ⑯ · ⑰ · Meth · Church · Hill Cottages · ⑬ · broken wall · The Heads · ⑪ · ★ · N · ⑩ · ⑱ · ⑲ · Northdale Beck · Blakey Ridge · Ironstone Railway · depression · right-of-way · Thorgill · Low Thorgill · ⑥ · ⑤ · ④ · heather · ★ · ★ · Gill Bank · Daleside Road (tarmac) · R. Seven · ⑦ · ③ · Castleton · Egton · shaft o Sheriff's Pit · ⑧ · Waterhouse Well · ① · ② · ROSEDALE ABBEY · Hutton-le-Hole · Pickering · Milburn Arms

fragment of Rosedale Priory

54

crosswall, then take level course across next field to a gate. (19)► Bear R down to ladder-stile at field corner and follow riverside path back to village.

ROSEDALE ABBEY

Many a tourist must have arrived at this little village expecting to find a majestic ruin à la Rievaulx or Fountains. There isn't one, though there was once a small priory, of which just a tiny fragment (a turret with a spiral staircase) remains standing near the church. The priory was founded c 1158 as a Cistercian nunnery and was dedicated to St. Mary and St. Lawrence. The priory chapel survived the Dissolution of 1538 and remained in use for public worship until 1839, when it was dismantled and replaced by the present, larger church. WATERHOUSE WELL, now covered by a low stone shelter, was a source of water for the nuns.

Waterhouse Well

ruins of pithead winding-house

The **IRONSTONE RAILWAY**, a magnificent feat of engineering, operated between 1861 and 1929, and transported, in its peak years, over a thousand tons of ore a day across the moors. The trackbed, now a permissive right-of-way, contours the valley heads in sweeping curves and is a walkers' delight. SHERIFF'S PIT, which was worked from 1857 to 1911, was one of Rosedale's most important mines. The ore was hauled coal mine-style up a 270 ft. shaft, which is now fenced and deeply flooded. Nearby stand the stark remnants of the pithead winding-house.

O.S. MAPS : Landranger Series (1:50 000) Sheet 100 (Malton and Pickering)   Outdoor Leisure 26 (1:25 000) SW Sheet

© Jack Keighley 1993

22

THREE CLEVELAND HEIGHTS

6¾ MILES

A dramatic walk along the rim of the precipitous escarpment overlooking the vast Cleveland Plain. The going is strenuous, with three separate steep climbs involving a total ascent of some 1200 feet. Though the walk is on clear paths throughout, it should be undertaken on a fine, clear day — ideally in late summer or autumn, when the colours are quite exquisite.

The Wainstones

55

DONNA CROSS

This socket stone lies by the path in the col between Cold Moor and Cringle Moor. It once carried a wayside cross which marked the route from Kirkby in Cleveland into Bilsdale. Carved upon it are the letters 'E' and 'F' to mark the boundaries of the Emmerson and Feversham estates.

ROUTE DIRECTIONS ① From car park walk L up road towards Helmsley. ② When forest on R ends, turn R up stepped path (cw sign). On reaching seat turn L over stile (acorn sign) and take broad path climbing steeply R through bracken. At top of climb a broad track continues forward along edge of escarpment. ③ Descend past The Wainstones (there are many paths and climbers' tracks. The simplest route lies to the R of all the rocks). Follow broad track down to depression and steeply up to top of Cold Moor. Keep straight on past summit cairn, then descend steeply to gate (acorn sign) in crosswall. ④ Follow broken wall on R round to gate/stile. (To shorten walk here see note below map) For full walk turn L along path with wall on L. When wall turns away keep straight on to cross tiny stream. ⑤ Follow path over spoil heaps and steeply up Cringle Moor. Path continues around rim of escarpment to seat and topograph at Cringle End (At the time of writing, work was due to begin on surfacing this path with stones and paving slabs). ⑥ Turn L at Cringle End to descend broad track with wall on R. ⑦ Pass through gate/stile and immediately turn back R over stile onto a broad green track. Where it forks take either branch – they soon re-join. Continue on clear path running more or less level along hillside. ⑧ Path eventually joins outward route. Turn L to retrace steps as far as Donna Cross, then fork L to follow path to stile (wm) at RH corner of plantation. Follow broad track forward along top edge of plantation. ⑨ At seat and stile leave forest road. Stay by wall on R to descend stepped path used at start of walk.

CRINGLE MOOR is the second highest point on the North York Moors, inferior only to Round Hill on Urra Moor (Walk 1). The summit, to which there is no official right-of-way, lies in a sea of heather 200yds to the south of the track and is marked by a large, untidy cairn atop a tumulus.

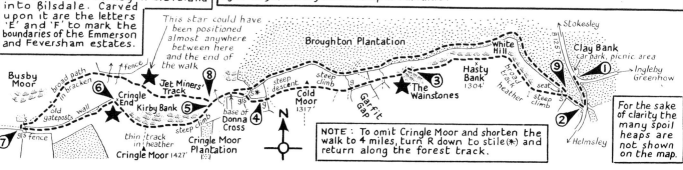

This star could have been positioned almost anywhere between here and the end of the walk

Broughton Plantation

Stokesley

White Hill

Clay Bank car park, picnic area

Ingleby Greenhow

Busby Moor

broad path in bracken

fence

Jet Miners' Track

Cringle End

old gateposts

wall

Kirby Bank

thin track in heather

Cringle Moor Plantation

Cringle Moor 1427

steep climb

base of Donna Cross

steep descent

steep climb

Cold Moor 1317

Garfit Gap

The Wainstones

Hasty Bank 1304

heather

broad track

seat

steep climb

B1257

Helmsley

N

NOTE: To omit Cringle Moor and shorten the walk to 4 miles, turn R down to stile (✱) and return along the forest track.

For the sake of clarity the many spoil heaps are not shown on the map.

THE WAINSTONES

is a great place to be. This jumble of sandstone crags and boulders is the largest group of rocks in the National Park, and the oddly-shaped pinnacles which serrate the skyline can be seen for miles around. Climbers abound. The photograph from which the drawing on the title page was done captured three - two relaxing on top of the rocks and their friend, below, otherwise engaged and blissfully unaware that he was being recorded for posterity.

seat, topograph and boundary stone, Cringle End.

JET MINING

Lines of spoil heaps along the hillsides tell of the industry of the jet miners of Victorian times. Jet is the fossilised wood of monkey-puzzle trees which flourished in these parts some 160 million years ago. Coal-like in appearance, it is easily carved and polished, and has been used for brooches, necklaces and ornaments since prehistoric times. Mining reached its zenith in the 1870s, but by the turn of the century jet was out of fashion and the industry had collapsed. 19th.C miners drove levels into the hillside, but the seams were thin and success was unpredictable.

A REQUEST
FROM THE HOLIDAY FELLOWSHIP

FRIEND, WHEN YOU STRAY, OR SIT AND TAKE YOUR EASE

ON MOOR OR FELL, OR UNDER SPREADING TREES

PRAY, LEAVE NO TRACES OF YOUR WAYSIDE MEAL,

NO PAPER BAG, NO SCATTERED ORANGE PEEL

NOR DAILY JOURNAL LITTERED ON THE GRASS

OTHERS MAY VIEW THESE WITH DISTASTE AND PASS

LET NO ONE SAY, AND SAY IT TO YOUR SHAME

THAT ALL WAS BEAUTY HERE BEFORE YOU CAME

plaque on the topograph

O.S. MAPS : Landranger Series (1 : 50 000) Sheet 93 (Middlesbrough and Darlington). Outdoor Leisure 26 (1 : 25 000) NW Sheet

---

HOLE OF HORCUM

6 MILES

A highly scenic walk featuring two of the Park's most spectacular views. After descending into the stupendous Hole of Horcum, a vast, 400' deep natural hollow, the way lies through attractive wooded valleys and over colourful moorland to Skelton Tower. This picturesque ruin teeters on the very brink of Newton Dale, one of Britain's most dramatic gorges. Easy walking on good paths.

the path into the Hole of Horcum

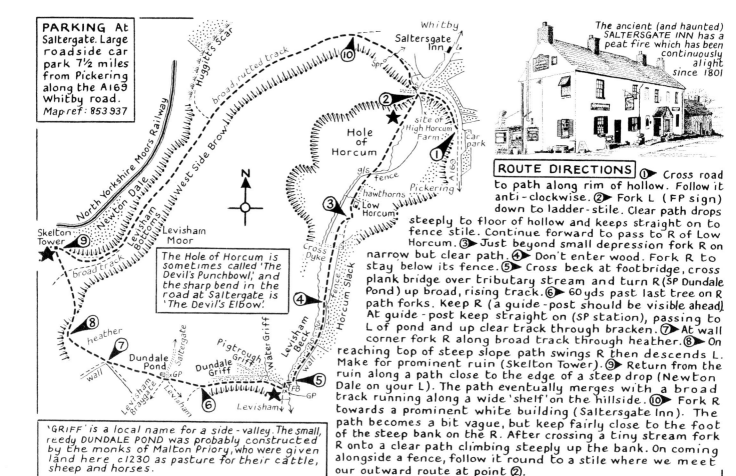

The ancient (and haunted) SALTERSGATE INN has a peat fire which has been continuously alight since 1801

The Hole of Horcum is sometimes called 'The Devil's Punchbowl,' and the sharp bend in the road at Saltergate is 'The Devil's Elbow!'

'GRIFF' is a local name for a side-valley. The small, reedy DUNDALE POND was probably constructed by the monks of Malton Priory, who were given land here c1230 as pasture for their cattle, sheep and horses.

ROUTE DIRECTIONS

①▶ Cross road to path along rim of hollow. Follow it anti-clockwise. ②▶ Fork L (FP sign) down to ladder-stile. Clear path drops steeply to floor of hollow and keeps straight on to fence stile. Continue forward to pass to R of Low Horcum. ③▶ Just beyond small depression fork R on narrow but clear path. ④▶ Don't enter wood. Fork R to stay below its fence. ⑤▶ Cross beck at footbridge, cross plank bridge over tributary stream and turn R (SP Dundale Pond) up broad, rising track. ⑥▶ 60 yds past last tree on R path forks. Keep R (a guide-post should be visible ahead). At guide-post keep straight on (SP station), passing to L of pond and up clear track through bracken. ⑦▶ At wall corner fork R along broad track through heather. ⑧▶ On reaching top of steep slope path swings R then descends L. Make for prominent ruin (Skelton Tower). ⑨▶ Return from the ruin along a path close to the edge of a steep drop (Newton Dale on your L). The path eventually merges with a broad track running along a wide 'shelf' on the hillside. ⑩▶ Fork R towards a prominent white building (Saltersgate Inn). The path becomes a bit vague, but keep fairly close to the foot of the steep bank on the R. After crossing a tiny stream fork R onto a clear path climbing steeply up the bank. On coming alongside a fence, follow it round to a stile where we meet our outward route at point ②.

THE HOLE OF HORCUM

Legend has it that this enormous depression, measuring ¾ mile across, was created when a giant named Wade grabbed a handful of earth to throw at his wife Bel. The soil, missing its target, landed a mile or so to the east to form the hill known as Blakey Topping. Geologists will tell you that in reality the Hole is the result of thousands of years of erosion by springs. There will be those who, like the author, may find the scientific explanation only marginally more believable than the legend. The Hole once contained two farmsteads — High and Low Horcum. The former was demolished in 1963. LOW HORCUM, built in 1811 and occupied until 1966, has been partially restored. The air currents rising from the hollow make this a popular venue for hang-gliders. In May 1976 Levisham Moor and the Hole of Horcum were purchased by the National Park Committee in order to conserve the beautiful landscape and retain public access.

* From Skelton Tower there is a truly magnificent view of the North Yorkshire Moors Railway sweeping through the wooded and steep-sided NEWTON DALE. This tremendous gorge — 11 miles long and 250 feet deep — was carved out by rushing torrents of glacial meltwater after the last Ice Age.

SKELTON TOWER was built as a shooting-lodge in 1850 by Rev. Robert Skelton, Vicar of Levisham. The National Park Authority did some restoration work to the ruin in 1978 in order to make it safe.

O.S. MAPS : Landranger Series (1:50 000) Sheet 100 (Malton and Pickering). Outdoor Leisure 27 (1:25 000) SE Sheet

© Jack Keighley 1993

A WOODLAND WALK FROM HELMSLEY

6¼ MILES

This unusual walk is one of several excellent rambles available from the lovely market town of Helmsley. It is an easy stroll, on good paths, through the mixed coniferous and deciduous woodlands which attractively clothe the 'twin' valleys of Ash Dale and Beck Dale. A useful walk to have 'on stand-by' for a dull, wet or misty day.

exit from Ash Dale Plantation

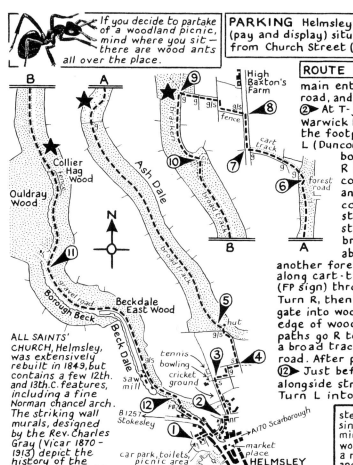

If you decide to partake of a woodland picnic, mind where you sit — there are wood ants all over the place.

PARKING Helmsley. Use the large, long stay car park (pay and display) situated near the castle and reached from Church Street (B1257 Stokesley). Map ref: 611 838

This scarecrow — a Frankenstein lookalike — was encountered just beyond point ⑥

ROUTE DIRECTIONS

①▶ From car park main entrance walk to Church Street, cross road, and continue along Canons Garth Lane. ②▶ At T-junction turn R, then L into Warwick Place. Keep straight ahead along the footpath, passing cricket ground on L (Duncombe Park C.C.) to reach stile (wm) by bowling club. ③▶ Cross stile and turn R to follow fence. Turn L at field corner, R through gate at next corner, and follow fence to reach a field corner with two stiles. ④▶ Take stile on L and follow fence to gate/stile into wood. ⑤▶ Turn L along broad forest track and follow it for about 1½ miles to a junction with another forest track. ⑥▶ Turn L to leave wood at a gate (wm). Continue along cart-track. ⑦▶ Turn R along tarmac road. ⑧▶ In 300 yds turn L (FP sign) through gate/stile and follow fence on L to field corner. Turn R, then L through gate/stile (FP sign). Follow fence on R to small gate into wood. ⑨▶ Turn sharp L to follow path through bracken near top edge of wood. Path eventually drops into small side-valley. ⑩▶ Two paths go R towards main valley. Take the LH (descending) one to reach a broad track running down valley bottom. ⑪▶ Bear L along gravel road. After passing a saw-mill on the R it becomes a tarmac lane. ⑫▶ Just before tarmac lane starts to climb, fork R onto narrow path alongside stream. Cross footbridge and follow stream to main road. Turn L into Helmsley.

ASH DALE

This narrow, steep-sided valley is known to have been wooded since at least the 16th C. Conifers and beech now mingle with trees more typical of the original woodland, such as oak, ash and hazel. Besides being a natural haven for butterflies and other insects, birds and small mammals, Ash Dale is rich in wild flowers.

ALL SAINTS' CHURCH, Helmsley, was extensively rebuilt in 1849, but contains a few 12th. and 13th.C. features, including a fine Norman chancel arch. The striking wall murals, designed by the Rev. Charles Gray (Vicar 1870-1913) depict the history of the church and parish.

Map labels: High Baxton's Farm, fence, cart track, forest road, broad track, bracken, Ash Dale, Collier Hag Wood, Ouldray Wood, N, Beckdale East Wood, Beck Dale, Borough Beck, gravel road, hut, tennis bowling cricket ground, saw mill, B1257 Stokesley, FB, car park, toilets, picnic area, Castle, HELMSLEY, market place, A170 Scarborough, A170 Thirsk, York

HELMSLEY

A marvellous little town – picturesque and colourful, warm and friendly, bustling and prosperous – at the centre of which is a MARKET SQUARE with a medieval cross and an ornate memorial to the Earl of Feversham. Helmsley caters comprehensively for tourists, and its fine selection of hotels and guest houses make it an ideal holiday centre. Dating back to pre-Norman times, and recorded as *Elmslac* in the Domesday Book, Helmsley developed into a thriving town when the CASTLE was built 1188-1227. The castle keep is, unusually, D-shaped, and its 8' thick walls are surrounded by impressive earthworks. In 1644, during the Civil War, the castle was besieged by roundhead troops for 3 months, and ultimately 'slighted' (i.e. rendered useless). Much of its stone was subsequently used for local building. To the W of the castle lies DUNCOMBE PARK, with its stately early 18th.C. mansion and formal gardens. In the 18th.C. Helmsley was an important flax linen-weaving centre. The town's population was then some 3,000, and regular stagecoach services left the famous old BLACK SWAN for Ripon, Richmond, York, Leeds and London.

THE [swan logo] HOTEL

O.S. MAPS : Landranger Series (1 : 50 000) Sheet 100 (Malton, Pickering). Outdoor Leisure 26 (1 : 25 000) SW Sheet

© Jack Keighley 1993

HEATHER MOORS OF UPPER RYEDALE

5½ MILES

For those who like lonely places and wide open spaces. An exhilarating circuit of the valley of Arns Gill, an early tributary of the Rye, following broad tracks along sweeping, purple ridges – the kind of country which epitomizes the National Park. A bright, clear day is needed to fully appreciate the beautiful views and rich colours.

cairn on Iron Howe

ROUTE DIRECTIONS

① Cross the white-railed bridge and walk along the road towards Hawnby for about a mile. ② When the road bends R, turn L along a farm road (sign - Private road to Scotland Farm). ③ When the farm road bends R, leave it and go forward up a grassy cart-track to a gate/stile. Continue up the ridge on a broad track which, beyond the cairn on Iron Howe, is provided with marker-posts. ④ Ignore a track heading R towards the T.V. mast. Stay on the main track which descends to cross Arns Gill before rising to an abandoned farm. ⑤ Track bends L at farm. Follow it up to cross a cattle-grid then head L along the broad ridge path. ⑥ Ignore a wide green path going off to the R. Keep straight on. Pass through gate in crosswall and follow track down to farm. ⑦ Turn R along farm access road and follow it down to gate. ⑧ Turn L down tarmac lane. ⑨ At road junction keep straight on (SP Hawnby 4¼ Helmsley 10½).

The **RIVER RYE** is born at Rye Head, on the moor some 2½ miles NW of Low Cote. We meet the river just as it commences the most beautiful section of its journey, for in passing through Hawnby, Rievaulx and Duncombe Park it flows through some of the loveliest countryside in England. Beyond Helmsley the Rye meanders lazily through meadowland to enter the Derwent at Rye Mouth, near Malton.

LIME KILNS

roadside lime kiln, Hall Lane

In the mid-18th century farmers began to build intake walls to enclose land on the edge of the moors. The new fields needed to be burned, drained and limed to neutralise the acid soils. Kilns were constructed to produce the huge amounts of lime required. A mixture of limestone and coal was fed into the top of the kiln and was fired by burning wood at the base. Once fired, the kiln would usually be kept going for 2 or 3 days, by which time it would have produced some 30-40 tons of lime - enough to treat about 6-8 acres of land. Lime burning ceased about 1860.

Head House

Arnsgill Ridge

grouse butts

× post

plank bridge

wall butts

broad track

Arns Gill

N

posts alongside track

Cow Ridge

grouse butts

Rye Farm

R. Rye

Hill End Farm

shapely cairn

Iron Howe

mounds of stones

Osmotherley

Low Cote

SNILESWORTH

Wheat Beck

R. Rye

RYE FARM · HILL END

Hall Lane

Plane Tree Farm

young plantation

kiln

gls

Lane House Farm

Hawnby

On Cow Ridge there are about 300 small mounds consisting almost entirely of small stones, together with traces of an ancient stone wall. Excavation has produced no evidence to support the theory that this was a prehistoric burial ground; the mounds remain a mystery.

62

SNILESWORTH is a district rather than a village — a scattered community of moorland farmsteads with no real focal point. —●-●-●—

The **BILSDALE T.V. MAST** dominates the view to the east. This BBC television transmitter, though certainly not a thing of beauty, is nevertheless a remarkable structure, which defies gravity with the assistance of a few cables. Inside the slender mast is a service lift which takes 7 minutes to take maintenance engineers up to the aerials 930 feet above Bilsdale West Moor.

GROUSE MOORS

Moorland such as we see on this walk accounts for about 40% of the National Park's total area, and constitutes the largest continuous tract of heather in England. This seemingly wild and wholly natural landscape is, in fact, closely controlled, for

HEAD HOUSE, a lonely, abandoned farm, now serves as a shooting house.

without careful management the heather would very soon deteriorate. The preservation is largely due to the popularity of the 'sport' of grouse-shooting. The red grouse (the only bird found exclusively in Britain) lives and breeds solely in this habitat, nesting and sheltering in the old heather and feeding on succulent young shoots. The male bird, darker than the female, has bright red wattles over his eyes during the breeding season. The chicks (usually 6-8) leave the nest immediately upon hatching and hide in the heather, where, should they survive predators and severe weather, they will face the guns from 12 August to 10 December. To encourage the growth of young 'food' shoots, patches of heather are burned in winter to destroy the old stems whilst leaving the roots intact.

O.S. MAPS : Landranger Series (1: 50 000) Sheet 100 (Malton and Pickering)   Outdoor Leisure 26 (1:25 000) SW Sheet

© Jack Keighley 1993

SANDSEND & KETTLENESS

6 MILES

The extensive quarrying of bygone days has left its mark without seriously marring the beauty of this fine, rocky section of the Heritage Coast. In fact, the industrial scars, which time and nature are slowly healing, enhance the interest of this breezy ramble. Apart from one short, very steep climb the walking is easy with sublime coastal views.

St. Oswald's Church, Lythe

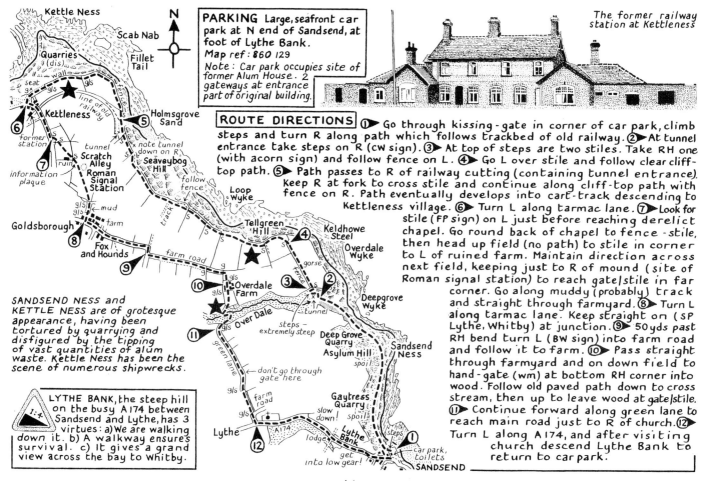

Kettle Ness

Scab Nab

Quarries (dis)

Fillet Tail

N

seat

Kettleness

Holmsgrove Sand

former station

tunnel

Scratch Alley Roman Signal Station

information plaque

note tunnel down on R

Seaveybog Hill

follow fence

Loop Wyke

mud

farm

track

Goldsborough

Fox and Hounds

farm road

Tellgreen Hill

Keldhowe Steel

Overdale Wyke

Overdale Farm

Over Dale

gorse

Deepgrove Wyke

steps – extremely steep

tunnel

green lane

Deep Grove Quarry

Asylum Hill

spoil

Sandsend Ness

don't go through gate here

farm road

Gaytress Quarry

spoil

Lythe

slow down!

A174

lodge

get into low gear!

Lythe Bank

steps

car park, toilets

SANDSEND

The former railway station at Kettleness

PARKING Large, seafront car park at N end of Sandsend, at foot of Lythe Bank.
Map ref: 860 129
Note: Car park occupies site of former Alum House. 2 gateways at entrance part of original building.

ROUTE DIRECTIONS ① Go through kissing-gate in corner of car park, climb steps and turn R along path which follows trackbed of old railway. ② At tunnel entrance take steps on R (CW sign). ③ At top of steps are two stiles. Take RH one (with acorn sign) and follow fence on L. ④ Go L over stile and follow clear cliff-top path. ⑤ Path passes to R of railway cutting (containing tunnel entrance). Keep R at fork to cross stile and continue along cliff-top path with fence on R. Path eventually develops into cart-track descending to Kettleness village. ⑥ Turn L along tarmac lane. ⑦ Look for stile (FP sign) on L just before reaching derelict chapel. Go round back of chapel to fence-stile, then head up field (no path) to stile in corner to L of ruined farm. Maintain direction across next field, keeping just to R of mound (site of Roman signal station) to reach gate/stile in far corner. Go along muddy (probably) track and straight through farmyard. ⑧ Turn L along tarmac lane. Keep straight on (SP Lythe, Whitby) at junction. ⑨ 50 yds past RH bend turn L (BW sign) into farm road and follow it to farm. ⑩ Pass straight through farmyard and on down field to hand-gate (wm) at bottom RH corner into wood. Follow old paved path down to cross stream, then up to leave wood at gate/stile. ⑪ Continue forward along green lane to reach main road just to R of church. ⑫ Turn L along A174, and after visiting church descend Lythe Bank to return to car park.

SANDSEND NESS and KETTLE NESS are of grotesque appearance, having been tortured by quarrying and disfigured by the tipping of vast quantities of alum waste. Kettle Ness has been the scene of numerous shipwrecks.

1:4 LYTHE BANK, the steep hill on the busy A174 between Sandsend and Lythe, has 3 virtues: a) We are walking down it. b) A walkway ensures survival. c) It gives a grand view across the bay to Whitby.

64

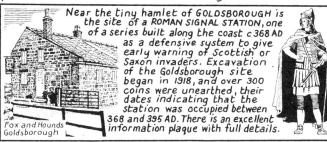

SANDSEND

is aptly named, for this little village, with its pretty cottages, stands at the northern extremity of 2½ miles of sandy beach from Whitby. It is hard to believe that this quiet little place was once a booming alum-quarrying and processing centre. The alum works closed down in 1867 after over 250 years of production. Today's visitor to Sandsend will discover a relaxing, non-commercialised holiday resort sheltered from cold northerly winds by the bare headland of Sandsend Ness.

DISASTER AT KETTLENESS On 17th. December 1829 torrential rain caused a cliff collapse which resulted in the entire village of Kettleness plunging into the sea. Fortunately the villagers were able to take refuge aboard 'Little Henry', an alum ship which happened to be lying just offshore. The present village – smaller than its predecessor – is still threatened by erosion.

Near the tiny hamlet of GOLDSBOROUGH is the site of a ROMAN SIGNAL STATION, one of a series built along the coast c 368 AD as a defensive system to give early warning of Scottish or Saxon invaders. Excavation of the Goldsborough site began in 1918, and over 300 coins were unearthed, their dates indicating that the station was occupied between 368 and 395 AD. There is an excellent information plaque with full details.

Fox and Hounds
Goldsborough

LYTHE CHURCH houses a display of fragments of carved stones – relics of a Danish burial ground of the 10th. C. All were found in the church walls during the 1910 rebuilding, and prove that a Christian church has stood here since at least 950 AD.

O.S. MAPS : Landranger Series (1 : 50 000) Sheet 94 (Whitby)
Outdoor Leisure 27 (1 : 25 000) NE Sheet

(27)

GREAT FRYUP HEAD

5¼ MILES

The precipitous slopes, beetling crags, cascading streams and waterfalls at the head of Great Fryup Dale blend delectably to create some of the most rugged scenery in the National Park. Apart from the short, steep climb out of the valley the walk is surprisingly easy – a gentle stroll along field paths, lanes and moorland tracks. The views down into Fryup Dale and Glaisdale are exceptionally beautiful.

A street corner

PARKING The narrow, enclosed lanes at the head of Great Fryup Dale are not conducive to parking cars. There are small roadside parking spaces at, and just above, the cattle-grid at Bainley Bank, SE of the hamlet of Street.

Map ref: 739 045

DO NOT PARK SO AS TO OBSTRUCT THE MOORLAND TRACKS

LOCATION MAP

(map labels: Danby, Houlsyke, Lealholm, Street, road signposted 'Fryup', Bainley Bank cattle-grid, Egton, Rosedale Abbey)

ROUTE DIRECTIONS ① Cross cattle-grid and walk down tarmac road. ② Fork R at road junction (*Fork L if you wish to take direct road route to Ajalon House, omitting Street*). Turn L (SP Danby 4) and walk through hamlet. ③ Take step-stile (FP sign) on L and bear slightly R across field to cross step-stile near gate. Turn R to RH of two gates and follow cart-track to farm. ④ Continue up-dale along tarmac road. ⑤ When valley road turns R, keep straight on along road with 'no through road' sign (Fryup Lodge only). Go through gate at end of road and cross beck. ⑥ Turn L along cart-track. ⑦ Follow track through gate and pass to R of barns. Cross tiny stream, and a few yards further on turn R up sunken green path. Re-cross tiny stream and head up through gap in broken wall to fence-stile. ⑧ Turn L and take thin path bearing slightly R away from fence. Path soon comes alongside wall on L. ⑨ When wall turns away, keep straight on, following thin path which maintains height, passes through gate in crosswall, then drops to stream in deep little valley. ⑩ Cross stream just below small ruin, go up far bank for 20yds then turn sharp R up clear path. This path gradually curves L to cross another stream. Turn R up green path parallel with stream. In about 100yds path turns L to climb very steeply, then R (detour here for view of waterfalls) up to large cairn at crosstrack. ⑪ Turn L along broad track. ⑫ Turn L down motor road. ⑬ At depression are FP and BW signs. Continue up road for a few more yards and turn L along broad track.

(map labels: Lealholm 3, small parking spaces, Great Fryup Beck, Street, Bainley Bank, Bainley Bank Cottage, valley road, Ajalon House, farm, right-of-way, broad track, Lealholm, Glaisdale Rigg, Hart Leap, Danby, valley road, Fryup Lodge, motor road, Rosedale, The Scar, The Hills a weird landscape, Oven Mouth, tin hut (an eyesore), ruin, Dale Head (barns), Wood Head, Great Fryup Beck, Yew Grain Scar, GP, Cut Road, broad track in heather, Trough House (visible on skyline), pile of stones, Great Fryup Head, Glaisdale Moor)

The OS map shows a public footpath from Hart Leap to Bainley Bank, and this is confirmed by a footpath sign at Hart Leap. However, there is no trace of a path in the deep heather, and the nearby broad track, which runs past Bainley Bank Cottage, is a better route (though not an official right-of-way).

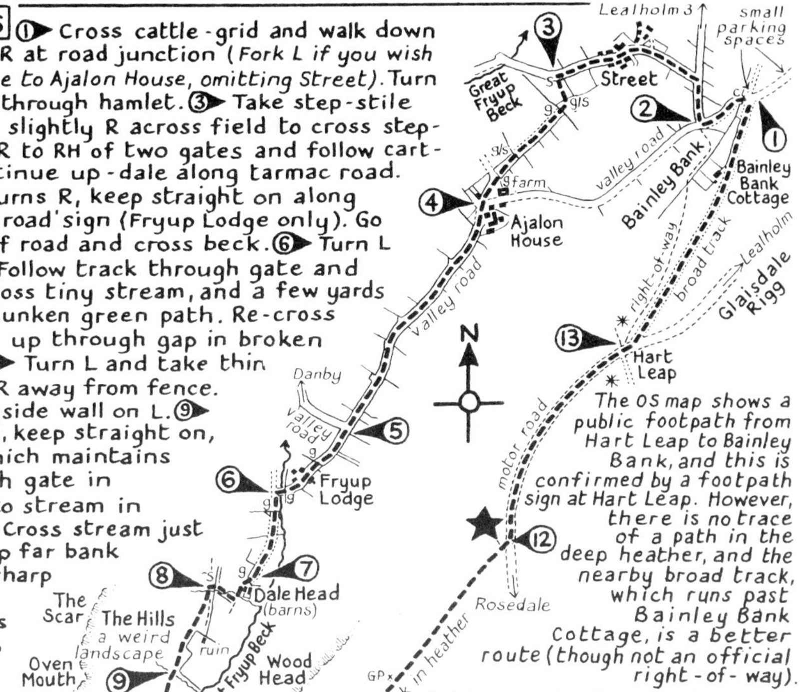

This splendid cairn on Glaisdale Rigg can be visited by a short detour up the road from point ⑬

Ajalon House

sign on gate near Ajalon House

BULL

Ajalon House was once well-known for it's Cleveland cheese, producing about 2 tons a year. Cheese-making on farms declined after the formation of the Milk Marketing Board, and ended altogether just after the Second World War.

BULLS AND THE LAW A farmer may put a beef bull (usually brown/red in colour) with a herd of cows in a field crossed by a public footpath. It is illegal to let a dairy bull (usually black and white) loose in a field open to public access.

Note the red deposit on the rocks around the water-falls — caused by iron in the water.

Bainley Bank Cottage

O.S. MAPS : Landranger Series (1:50 000) Sheet 94 (Whitby)
Outdoor Leisure 27 (1:25 000) NE Sheet

© Jack Keighley 1993

28

LOWNA & HARLAND MOOR

5 MILES

This easy Lower Farndale stroll is a walk for all seasons. April offers a chance to enjoy the famous daffodils without encountering huge crowds of tourists. Late summer transforms the moor into a sea of purple, and a sunny autumn day lends a golden glow to the bracken slopes. The views can be particularly splendid on a cold, crisp winter's morn.

Lowna Bridge

ROUTE DIRECTIONS ① From public car park turn L down road to cross Lowna Bridge and cattle-grid. ② 40 yds past cattle-grid turn L up wide track, and in 150 yds fork L (FP Low Mill) to follow broad path with wall on L. ③ On passing through gate into wood keep L on main track. Stay with it as it descends through wood, ignoring any paths branching off to R. ④ Just before reaching house turn L to cross footbridge then R up broad track. ⑤ From gate/stile take RH and narrowest of three paths. It runs through bracken close to river and comes alongside a wall briefly before climbing L to merge with path coming down out of wood. Keep on upstream to reach a footbridge. ⑥ Turn L up clear path, which climbs steeply before swinging R to run between fence and wall. Cross stile in fence on L and continue forward on broad track. ⑦ Just before track reaches crossfence it turns very sharp L and climbs hillside to stile in fence. Cross it and keep on up for about 80 yds to reach cart-track. Turn R along it, but keep a sharp look-out for a thin track (it starts near a silver birch) climbing L through heather. Path passes wall-corner to reach tarmac road at or near a pair of footpath signs. ⑧ Cross road and proceed along broad track (FP sign) through heather. Track eventually swings R to gate in wall. ⑨ Continue forward, with wall on L, and in 80 yds fork L through gate to footbridge/ford. ⑩ On crossing stream turn L up broad track. It soon comes alongside wall on L. Ignore first gap in this wall. Continue to gap at corner of broken walls, then bear L and make for gate. On passing through it take the RH path and descend through small conifers to small gate at bottom LH corner of field. ⑪ Turn L along tarmac road. ⑫ About 300 yds past entrance to Grays Farm turn L through gate (BW sign) onto cart-track. At bottom of field turn R to follow path between fence and hedge (BW sign). ⑬ Keep straight on along cart-track through trees. On emerging from wood fork R to follow farm track. ⑭ Turn L along road.

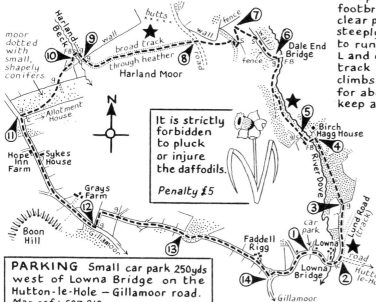

It is strictly forbidden to pluck or injure the daffodils.

Penalty £5

moor dotted with small, shapely conifers

Harland Beck

butts

broad track through heather

Harland Moor

wall

fence

Dale End Bridge FB

Allotment House

Hope Inn Farm

Sykes House

Grays Farm

Boon Hill

Gillamoor

Birch Hagg House

River Dove

Lund Road (track)

car park

Faddell Rigg

Lowna

Lowna Bridge

Hutton-le-Hole

road

PARKING Small car park 250 yds west of Lowna Bridge on the Hutton-le-Hole — Gillamoor road. Map ref: 687 910

Alternatively there is parking space 50 yds east of the bridge.

SYKES HOUSE

LOWNA FARM

enjoys an Arcadian setting on the banks of the Dove. Only a farmstead now, but the large building was once a busy tannery. Here also was a mill, where corn was ground and bones crushed to produce meal.

THE BIRDLIFE

of this wooded stretch of the valley of the Dove is rich and varied, and three interesting species to look out for are the heron, jay and long-tailed tit. If you are very quiet you may be lucky enough to come upon a HERON standing one-legged, hunched and motionless at the water's edge. When disturbed, this huge bird (it stands 3' tall) will flap away languidly in search of a more peaceful fishing site. The wary JAY will be more often heard than seen, for its harsh screech 'skaaark, skaark' is a familiar sound of the dense woodland in which this handsome member of the crow family prefers to live. The LONG-TAILED TIT may be seen in small flocks in more open woodland. This acrobatic little bird is only 5½" long - and 3" of that is tail!

Long-tailed tit

A LOWNA GHOST STORY

In 1787 two lovers, Willie Dixon and Kitty Garthwaite, quarrelled bitterly by the ford where Lowna Bridge now stands, and the next morning Kitty was found drowned in a deep pool below the ford. Her body, dressed only in a white sark (a kind of short underslip) was taken to the nearby mill, where it lay in a barn for two days. Willie learned of the tragedy on his return from York, where he had been to obtain a special licence to marry Kitty. He hastened to the barn, only to find that the body and the sark (which had been washed and hung up to dry) had mysteriously vanished. The following day Willie was found drowned in the same pool. There were many subsequent reports of Kitty being seen near the ford, naked and carrying a white sark, and hardly a year passed without a man being found drowned in the pool. Eventually the Vicar of Lastingham conducted a burial service at the scene, and since then the drownings have ceased and the ghost of Kitty has been seen no more.

O.S. MAPS : Landranger Series (1 : 50 000) Sheet 100 (Malton and Pickering).   Outdoor Leisure 26 (1 : 25 000) SW Sheet

© Jack Keighley 1993

INGLEBY INCLINE

7¼ MILES

A breezy upland walk starting from the superb little church at Ingleby Greenhow. Once the climb of some 400' from Bank Foot has been accomplished you may stride out briskly along the easy moorland track to the remarkable railway incline, which now provides a magnificent walkers' way off the tops. A great walk on a fine day, but exposed and unpleasant in bad weather.

the cairn on Burton Howe

PARKING Ingleby Greenhow. Parking space near the church. Map ref : 581 062

ROUTE DIRECTIONS (1) Walk up road away from church and at T-junction turn R (SP Kildale 3¼, Castleton 10½). (2) 25yds past telephone box turn R (FP sign). Follow path between fences to stile, then continue forward along LH edge of fields and through two more stiles. Continue forward across next field (initially with hedge and tiny stream on R). (3) Cross fence stile and turn sharp L (SP Bank Foot) through gate/stile and forward with fence on L to stile (wm). Follow LH side of hedge then, at a gap, cross to its RH side and continue forward to gate. (4) Turn R along tarmac lane. Keep straight on along it, ignoring a track branching R. Pass farm and go through gate to rough track climbing through plantation. Keep straight on (FP sign) at crosstracks. (5) Stay on main track through LH of two gates. Track eventually swings R to run SSE along the moor. (6) Look for some grouse butts along LH side of track. Just before second butt turn R onto a lesser path (not an official right-of-way, but a commonly-used short cut). (7) Turn R down a broad, sunken track (The Incline). At foot of Incline keep straight on along level cinder track. (8) At end of sparse woodland on L turn L over stile (wm) and go straight down fields to footbridge. (9) Cross bridge, turn L through gate/stile (wm) then turn R to climb RH side of two fields to tarmac lane. Turn R along it. (10) Turn R into Low Farm drive. Just before farm turn L (FP sign). Cross stile, turn R and then L along LH side of hedge. Cross stile and head across big field towards house. Stile in corner to L of it. (11) Straight on across drive to stile. Cross big field, gradually nearing trees on R. Cross fence-stile and follow edge of wood. (12) Through small gate, down steps (may be slippery) and turn R.

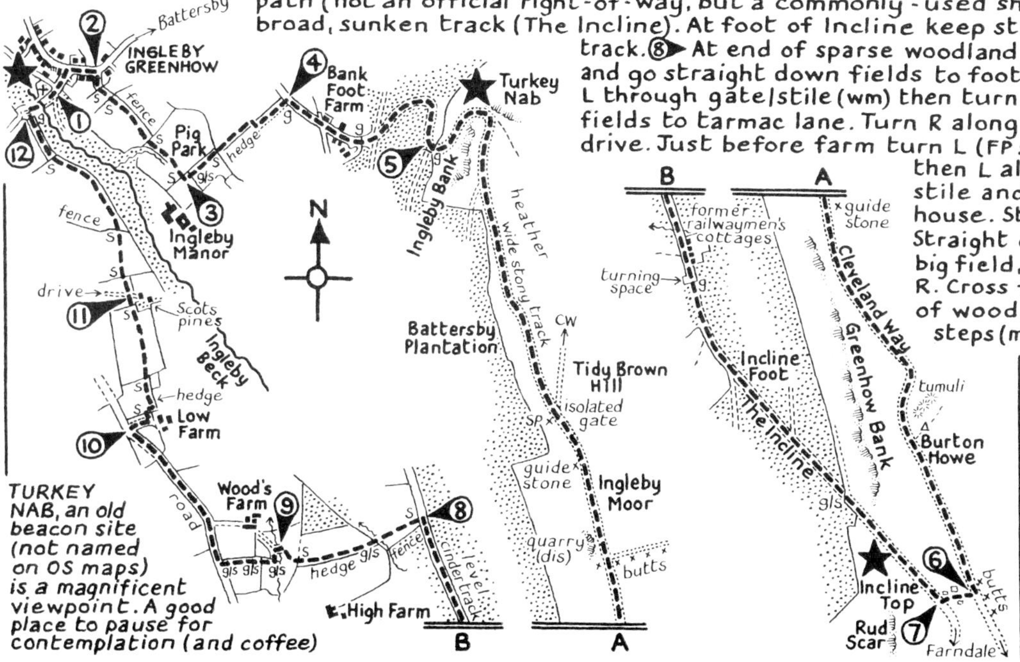

Battersby
INGLEBY GREENHOW
Bank Foot Farm
Turkey Nab
Pig Park
hedge
fence
Ingleby Manor
Ingleby Bank
heather
wide stony track
N
drive
Scots pines
Ingleby Beck
Battersby Plantation
CW
Tidy Brown Hill
isolated gate
guide stone
Ingleby Moor
quarry (dis)
butts
hedge
Low Farm
road
Wood's Farm
hedge
fence
level cinder track
High Farm
B
A
former railwaymen's cottages
guide stone
turning space
Cleveland Way
Greenhow Bank
Incline Foot
The Incline
tumuli
Burton Howe
Incline Top
Rud Scar
Farndale
butts

TURKEY NAB, an old beacon site (not named on OS maps) is a magnificent viewpoint. A good place to pause for contemplation (and coffee)

This isolated gate stands at the point where our route joins the Cleveland Way. 250yds further on, on the R, is an ancient way-marker stone (Greenhow Road).

Cleveland Way signpost

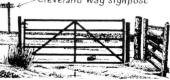

INGLEBY GREENHOW is an attractive little village enjoying a sheltered situation at the foot of the steep Cleveland escarpment. The earliest known reference to the manor of 'Englebi' is in the Domesday Survey (1086), though there is no mention of a church existing here at that time.

ST. ANDREW'S
INGLEBY GREENHOW
● — ● — ● — ●

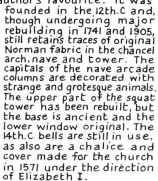

Of all the many lovely churches in the North York Moors, this little gem is the author's favourite. It was founded in the 12th.C and, though undergoing major rebuilding in 1741 and 1905, still retains traces of original Norman fabric in the chancel arch, nave and tower. The capitals of the nave arcade columns are decorated with strange and grotesque animals. The upper part of the squat tower has been rebuilt, but the base is ancient and the lower window original. The 14th.C bells are still in use, as also are a chalice and cover made for the church in 1571 under the direction of Elizabeth I.

The tall GUIDE STONE to the left of the moorland track is a fine specimen, inscribed with directions (interesting spelling), hands and the date 1757.

● ● BURTON HOWE IS A BRONZE AGE BURIAL SITE ● ●

THE INCLINE lifted the Ironstone Railway (built 1861) to the moor top. Wagons were raised and lowered 729' in less than a mile by cable attached to a steam winding-engine. The last load of iron ore went down the Incline 11-1-1929.

O.S. MAPS : Landranger Series (1:50 000) Sheets 93 (Darlington) and 94 (Whitby)   Outdoor Leisure 26 (1:25 000) NW Sheet
© Jack Keighley 1993

(30)

GORMIRE LAKE & THE WHITE HORSE

5¾ MILES

A classic walk visiting two of the Park's most famous features – the enchanting Gormire Lake and the amazing White Horse of Kilburn. Connecting the two is a spectacular track along the rim of the 200' high cliffs forming the Hambleton escarpment, with magnificent views to the west. Try to avoid summer weekends and Bank Holidays, when the locality seethes with tourists.

JKeighley

White Horse of Kilburn

Cleveland Way
wall
8
9
broken fence
wooden walkway
Whitestone Cliff
broken wall
Great Relief
Garbutt Wood
Pot
Cliff Plantation
private
Cold Kirby
SUTTON BANK INFORMATION CENTRE
displays, bookshop, refreshments, toilets
nature trail
Sutton Brow
7
Gormire Lake
Gormire Farm
→Helmsley
10
Kilburn Moor Plantation
High Rigg
farm road
N
Sutton Bank
Valley View
Castern Dike
Thirsk
A170
A170
6
farm road
Hood Grange Farm
Happy Valley
5
huge field
information board
ignore path descending R
railed path
forest road
Yorkshire Gliding Club
4
Hood Hill
3
Roulston Scar
forest road
runway
The Iron Age earthworks on Hood Hill's summit are discernible from the top of Roulston Scar. Hood Grange Farm stands on the site of a small monastery used by the Cistercians (1138-43) and Augustinians (1145-1332)
Ivy Scar
11
telescope (20p)
White Horse
seat
2
forest road
large car park
White Horse Bank
(tarmac lane)
tower
small car park
deer enclosure
farm
1
→Oldstead
Kilburn

PARKING White Horse Bank, on the road running north from Kilburn to the A170. There are two convenient car parks – a small, little-used one at the foot of the bank and a large one immediately below the White Horse. The walk is described as starting from the former. Map ref: 514 807

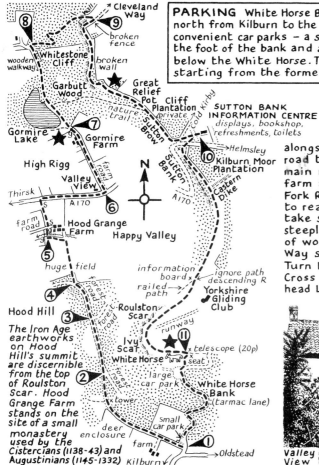

ROUTE DIRECTIONS ① Go down road towards Kilburn, and in 40 yds turn R along farm road (bridleway sign). When farm road turns L to farm leave it and keep straight on along green track. ② Green track joins forest road. Keep straight on along it. ③ At Y-junction of forest roads take L fork (straight on). ④ Just before road swings L at forest edge turn R (bridleway sign) on path to leave forest. Head straight across big field (clear path), and at farm turn L (blue arrow) alongside fence. ⑤ Turn R through gate (bridleway sign). Cross farm road to facing ladder-stile and go straight up field. Turn R along main road. ⑥ Turn L up farm road (bridleway sign). Pass to R of farm and continue alongside hedge to gate overlooking lake. ⑦ Fork R to follow clear path passing to R of lake. Keep straight on to reach boardwalk across boggy area. ⑧ When boardwalk ends take second path on R (SP Thirlby Bank). Clear, sunken path winds steeply up through wood (with occasional bridleway signs). At top of wood keep straight on up to reach crosstrack with Cleveland Way sign. ⑨ Turn R to follow broad path along rim of escarpment. Turn L at far end of plantation to visit Information Centre. ⑩ Cross main road and fork R to visit topograph above Sutton Bank, then head L along broad path by plantation. Follow this path along top of escarpment to arrive at White Horse. ⑪ Turn R to descend stepped path to car park, and R again down tarmac lane to small car park.

Valley View

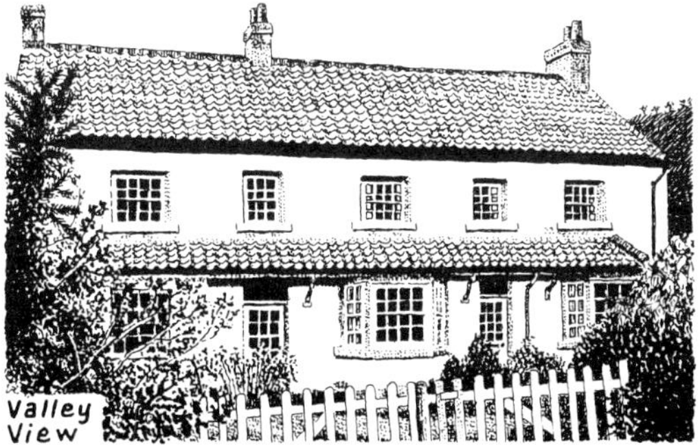

Sections ①-②, ④-⑤ and ⑧-⑨ liable to be muddy. The clifftop path between Whitestone Cliff and the White Horse is NO PLACE FOR LARKING ABOUT. Children should be closely supervised.